CANINE AND ABLED™
Taking The Dis Out of Disabled

CANINE AND ABLED™

Taking The Dis Out of Disabled

Kimberly Carnevale

Copyright © 2004 by Kimberly Carnevale.

Library of Congress Number:		2004094146
ISBN:	Hardcover	1-4134-5827-0
	Softcover	1-4134-5826-2

All rights reserved. No part of this book may be reproduced, stored in a retrieval system, or transmitted by any means, electronic, mechanical, photocopying, recording, or otherwise without expressed written permission from the author.

This book was printed in the United States of America.

To order additional copies of this book, contact:
Xlibris Corporation
1-888-795-4274
www.Xlibris.com
Orders@Xlibris.com
23443

This work is dedicated first,
to my precious daughter Sarah.
Everything I do, I do for you,
my precious little angel.
To my dogs:
You are my freedom and so much more…
With you by my side,
I've embarked upon a magical journey,
which is still unfolding.
You have taken me to a level of recovery
that no doctor or medication could achieve;
for that, and for all that you do—I am truly grateful.
I'm humbled by your love and devotion to me,
and feel honored to hold a place in your hearts.
I love you,
THANK YOU!

Acknowledgements

This book is a step in a most-incredible journey, one that is still unfolding. I thought my accident ended my life; what I've discovered is that a new one was just beginning; one filled with many gifts. I've been led down a miraculous path, one that has challenged me to the core of my existence, rewarded me beyond my wildest expectations, and lifted me up to a deeper appreciation and understanding of this thing we call 'life'.

First and foremost, I thank God, for giving me the opportunity to try to be the person that He wants me to me, and showing me the strength we all have inside. I pray daily that I remain in light and truth and live up to His expectations and that I am able to make a difference with the second chance I've been given.

To my precious baby daughter, Sarah . . . You are the cherry on the cake of my life! You are the child I'd ached for and dreamed of having, but was told I couldn't due to medical complications; you are truly my miracle baby! Praise God! . . . There are no words that could begin to express how much I love, cherish, and am amazed by you. Your mere existence proves what I've always believed, and that is if we walk on a spiritual path, and have faith in everything we do; we are rewarded far beyond our expectations. Just when I thought my life was full again, you burst into it and brought to me a love that is earth shattering and unexplainable. I love looking at life through your eyes . . . each day bringing something new and exciting . . . For nine magical months, you grew under my heart; now you live in it and fill up every inch of it! Everyday with you is a dream come true; and everything I do, I do for you . . . Being your Mommy is an honor and a privilege; and I vow to be the very best. You are truly Heaven's Gift! God bless you always, my precious little angel.

Unending thanks to my entire family, especially my parents who always stood by me not matter what. Daddy, I love you and miss you, yet I know you are watching over me . . . You taught me so much, both in your life and your death . . . tools I have used to get through this most-difficult ordeal. Thank you for always being there for me; even now . . . Mom, since my accident, you have been by my side every step of the way. Thank you for all the selfless chores, unending love, and endless compassion; I couldn't have gotten through this without you. You have set a wonderful example of what it is to be a great Mom. I know I'm going to be a great Mom to her because I had a great teacher! I love you so much! Thank you! To my brother, Rick, thank you for always supporting me, no matter what I was going through. You've always stood by me, as a big brother should. We've had a lot of fun together, yet I know that this all has been rough on you, even though you never let on. You are a great Uncle to Sarah and a great brother to me. I love you! Thanks for all the hockey games; they were lots of fun! Lookin' forward to seeing the green birds fly all the way! (Let's go Eagles!) To Keith and Mark; I still think back to when we were all kids living together as a family . . . and miss it horribly . . . I think about Christmastime when we were little and you guys would be up all night wrapping presents and putting up the tree so that Ricky and I would be surprised in the morning. I could never figure out why you were so tired on Christmas day! I think about the street hockey games, playing spot at night, and swimming until we were waterlogged . . . I miss those simpler times so much . . . Then I think about your own families and realize that things move on and get bigger and better! Julie, Sean, Nicholas, Luba, Zachary and Max are proof of that . . . I love you all!

To Eileen; my soul-sister and boot-scootin' buddy: Look up "best friend" in the dictionary, and there you are! You are what best friends are all about. From Sunday school to middle school, high school to the school of life, you have always stood by me whatever happened. For that, and for all that you are and all that you do; I am eternally grateful. Thank you doesn't seem to say what I feel when I look back at all you've done for me. You've always believed in me; even when I didn't believe in myself . . . I want you to know, I believe in you, too! Thank you for sticking by me when it wasn't an easy thing to do. Sarah couldn't have a better Godmother . . . . and I couldn't have a better friend. I love you!

To *all* my friends, including my "dance associates" : Susan, Nancy, Sue M., Kelly, Anne, Steve(s), Jeff, and Amy, "my buddy," Shelly, DJ Joe White, DJ "Marky-Mark," and the *entire* Prospector's gang, the *entire* Champion's Meadow crew, and my fellow "barn rats," thanks to you for all your help and support (you know who you are!)

To everyone at Ri-Arm Farm, including but not limited to; Jane, Allison, Steve, Armand and Peter. I'd be remiss if I didn't send out a special thanks to my coach, Mark Leone. Thank you for believing in Slack and me and giving us a chance at the big time . . . You took a chance on a kid from nowhere who rode a horse that came from the same place. I may not have had the best of trainers growing up (heck, until you, I didn't have any!) and Slack may not have had the best pedigree or confirmation; but what we lacked in those areas, we made up for in drive and ambition. You looked beyond our financial limitations and saw the hunger in both our eyes. You saw a horse that would jump the moon if I asked him to, simply because he loved me . . . . You recognized my unquenchable thirst for knowledge and offered me every opportunity to learn, grow, and try to attain the goals that others merely scoffed at. While I may not have achieved my ultimate victory of Olympic Gold, (I told you I've always been looking to take your job! (Grin), I believe I have come away with even more . . . the respect of a rider, coach, and friend who believed in me and my dreams. Thank you. Win a gold for me, okay?

To Emmy . . . aka, the Nanny . . . aka, Opare, aka, Chief keep 'er outta trouble and in clean, dry, pants, childcare provider: Thanks for sitting on boot-scootin' nights! In all seriousness, I could not have finished this book without your help. Sarah and I would like to thank you from the bottom of our hearts for all your assistance. Best of luck to you and Tyler . . . . we have faith and believe in both of you and your dream . . . . now believe in yourself and get out there and make it come true!

To Pastor Gromest . . . thanks for all your support and encouragement and helping me to find the "something" that I was desperately searching for. Dewey and Dawson thank you for the Milkbones®!

To Don . . . from the first C&A program, you believed in me and believed in what I was trying to accomplish. Thanks so much for your dedication, selfless assistance, and wonderful advice; God bless.

To Jerry and Tommy and my beloved godsons, Kyle and Matthew, my life is blessed with you in it . . . I love you!

To Canine and Abled™ audiences and supporters . . . you heard my call to end access denials and answered in hearty unison. Your support has been overwhelming and unending. Thank you.

To the paramedics, doctors, and all health care professionals . . . thank you for saving me, easing my pain and teaching me how to live again. Your job is not an easy one and is often overshadowed by tragedy and loss. I don't know how you do it, but just keep doing it!

To my dogs, (and I include my late Brandy, who although she wasn't a service dog, cared for me after my accident in a way that would do any service dog proud . . . she is cherished in a love that transcends time). . . . . You have been a beacon of hope in the darkness of my despair and because of your light; I am able to see a bright future. Tomorrow is no longer dreaded, but anticipated with great expectations of a new life . . . I can't wait to see how it turns out! You give so much; yet never ask anything in return. You have taught me so much, about life, about faith, and myself. I love you . . . THANK YOU!

Forward

It is with great pride that I write this forward for my dear friend Kim, whom I have known for many years and have grown to admire for her strength and dedication to realizing her dream.

My name is Mark Leone, and I have been in the equestrian world for 30 years perusing my dream of being a world-class show jumping rider. I have been fortunate enough to represent the United States all over the world and teach young equestrians the art of show jumping.

I met Kim many years ago at a horse show and she wanted to come and work with me to pursue her riding career and learn horse management. Kim had a good talent and a real zest for the sport. Several months in to her job Kim developed Lyme disease and it was the beginning of a new battle that we both felt she could overcome. Kim returned home to treat this illness with the understanding that she would return to work when she was better. It seemed we had a good plan.

It was then that Kim faced another big hurdle to clear. While Kim was treating her Lyme disease, she was in a devastating car accident that would again change her life. Kim sustained severe damage to her neck and back as well as her brain. She was wheelchair bound for about two years and has been rehabilitating herself. She has been relentless in her quest to resume a normal life.

Through this tragic event, Kim has sort out innovative ways to better herself and that's where she learned the great value and need of canine assistance. The canine's ability to assist disabled persons in rehabilitation is quite remarkable. Through this relationship, Kim has been steadily improving and is out of her wheelchair and is walking and resuming her life to the best of her ability. She has great confidence in herself and her future.

In closing, it is quite inspiring to me to see how a person faced with life threatening events can conquer these problems. Kim is a big canine advocate who believes that a person with disabilities can overcome these obstacles and realize their dream.

Mark Leone
USET Show Jumping Rider
Coach/friend

Canine and Abled™—How It All Began . . .

"Being partnered with a service dog has opened my eyes to a gross misunderstanding throughout the general public about service dogs, their partner's rights and the unique benefits these wonderful animals provide for their partners. These misunderstandings lead to access denials and rude behavior being imposed upon many teams throughout the service dog community.

For persons who rely upon the assistance of service dogs, public awareness can mean the difference between free access and senseless (and illegal) harassment.

Canine and Abled™ provides explanations of laws that pertain to service dog teams, business rights and obligations, etiquette and more.*

It is my fervent hope that my audience members will take these lessons with them and apply them in their everyday lives, thereby holding open doors for all persons who rely upon the assistance of service dogs."-Kimberly Carnevale

*   Disclaimer: Canine and Abled™ is NOT a law service. We only offer brief explanations and interpretations of service dog law as is readily available from published sources. Those seeking legal advice should contact a licensed attorney.

What IS Canine and Abled™?

Canine and Abled™ is a program dedicated to promoting acceptance of service dog teams everywhere. This goal is achieved through motivational speaking, ADA and disability rights workshops, and service dog education. Programs will benefit any group. Some examples of Canine and Abled™ audiences are: businesses, schools, civic organizations, churches, boy/girl scouts & more!

Kimberly Carnevale is the founder and president of Canine and Abled™. A professional athlete until 1998 when a car accident left her permanently disabled, Kimberly has overcome her challenges and devotes her time to service dog and disability advocacy. In addition to being an author and teaching about the benefits of service dogs, she also shares her incredible story in the form of a motivational seminar.

"I'd be remiss if I didn't share the lessons I've learned on this incredible journey; lessons I promise will change your life, much as they have mine. When my audiences hear my story and learn how I was able to overcome what I've been through, they walk away knowing that the ability and tools needed to realize their dreams already lies within themselves. When faced with seemingly insurmountable challenges, we all have two choices-we can let them beat us down or use them to make us stronger. I choose to be strong!"

—Kimberly Carnevale

Prologue

The force of the impact was incredible. Glass shattered around me, raining down everywhere. The sickening, crunching sound of metal was deafening and I felt myself spinning. I saw the taillights in front of me disappear and then the headlights of the cars that were behind me were heading at me; and so it continued. I was spinning forever, it seemed. I was saying a silent prayer. I was wishing blessings on my family and friends because I knew I was about to die. There was no pain. I was surprised. That would come later; I was to learn. It was amazing just how many thoughts went through my head in that seemingly very small amount of time. The noise stopped and the spinning stopped. It was quiet; too quiet. My thoughts were thrust into darkness, and then they drifted to a simpler time, one filled with comforting memories of a lifetime of striving for the ultimate goal of Olympic Gold.

It's taken me a long time to write this. There was a time, not so long ago, when the words would spew from my mind and travel through my fingertips to quickly fill the void of an empty page. The accident changed all that. It not only changed what I did—it changed who I am.

Lately I've felt the old, familiar stirrings of my writer's mind—a welcome visit from a dear, old friend who had been away far too long. You see; I had to relearn to read and write to create this work. The words and feelings are different, no so carefree as before, yet the need is the same. The need is to capture my thoughts and feelings on an empty page and paint living, breathing images with the strokes of my keyboard. I yearn again to mesh those feelings with the perfect descriptions, so as to transport, you, my reader into another place and time. My keyboard is your roadmap and my words are the tour that will guide you through an unforgettable journey. My life has been a tumultuous journey; one that has been filled with excitement, heartaches, excruciating pain, and finally; hope and joy. It is a journey that is still unraveling, slowly leading me to my destiny. I invite you to share in this journey and hope that by taking this trip with me, you'll be able see how our challenges in life are often blessings in disguise.

Chapter One

"He bounds from the earth; when I bestride him, I soar, I am a hawk. He trots the air; the earth sings when he touches it."—William Shakespeare. That ultimately freeing, totally gratifying, four-footed bliss one can only experience from the back of a horse was what I lived for. Feeling at one with a thousand-pound animal proved to be the driving force in my life. I don't remember ever not riding; it was innate, like breathing.

I was adopted into a non-horse, middle-class, suburban home as an infant. I was blessed with two great parents who loved and respected my siblings and I, and did everything in their power to give us the world. I have an older brother who was also adopted, and two older cousins that my parents were guardians for after my father's sister was killed. We were all raised as one family unit with old-fashioned morals and were given a strong sense of family early on. It was important to my parents that we thought of each other as brothers and sister, and put the adoptions in the back of our minds. It worked. I felt lucky and blessed to have been integrated into such a warm, loving home.

I was the youngest and only girl, which gave me a great advantage of learning from my older brother and cousins the intricacies of climbing trees, fixing my own bicycle chain, catching a fish, riding dirt bikes and other tomboy activities. I never was a 'typical' young lady. My wardrobe consisted of blue jeans and t-shirts instead of dresses. I never played with dolls. They bored me. I preferred my stuffed animals, or better yet, live ones.

From an early age, I had an intense need to be around animals. I was forever bringing home stray and injured animals, much to my mother's chagrin. I brought home everything! A bird with a broken wing, a turtle with a broken shell, or a dog who was lost and hungry; if it needed help, I brought it home. Finally Mom had had enough. It got to a point that whenever I'd head for the front door, she'd sternly tell me, "Don't bring home anything home that has feathers, fur, fins, or scales!" That didn't stop me, though. Thinking about what a hurt, lost, or abandoned animal would go through without my help convinced me that an admonishment from Mom was well worth the price of helping an animal in need.

Meeting a few new "friends"

My parents were constantly amazed and amused by the way I interacted with animals. "It was almost as if she spoke their language," My mother often tells stories of my "animal magnetism," which surfaced very early in my life. There was this one time when I was about five years old, visiting with my grandparents. They took me to their weekend lake house where they met up with another couple to play cards. I'm told that at first, I was disheartened because there were no other children to play with, but my mood brightened considerably when I saw the host family had a dog. Immediately, I went to introduce myself, but was brought up short by his owner's panicked warning. "He bites," she explained to my grandmother. "He really dislikes children and won't go to anyone, not even my husband!" I was sad that I couldn't play with the cute little dog, so my grandmother took me into the other room and set me up with some crayons and drawing paper. Meanwhile, she returned to her card game and reminded me to stay away from the dog. Some time later when she came to check on me, she and her friends got quite the surprise when they saw the little dog curled up in my lap, sound asleep. "I thought we told you not to go near that dog," my grandmother admonished. "I didn't, Grandma. He came to me! We're friends now!"

Friends. That's how I've always characterized the animals that choose to spend their time with me. I understood them, and they understood me, better than anyone. It was a gift that I cherished from the start. It was a gift that came with responsibility, I knew, and I took that responsibility very seriously. Animals were people too, I always believed. They were just wrapped differently!

One of my closest childhood friends was a Britney Spaniel named Rusty. I was eight-years old when my father bought Rusty for my brother as a hunting dog. With great breeding and a long line of hunting bloodlines, he was sure to be a great gun dog. That is, until I got involved. We brought Rusty home as an eight-week old puppy. My father was told that in order to be a good hunting dog, a pup needed to live in a kennel, not in the house with the family, as that would lead to spoiling him. I think that plan lasted all of ten seconds. Once I'd heard that Daddy planned to keep that tiny puppy outside, I pulled out the big guns; I went to Mom. She agreed that no little puppy should be left alone in a kennel, so it was agreed (begrudgingly), that Rusty would live inside. There was the stipulation that he was to sleep in the kitchen in his own bed, however. That plan lasted a bit longer—right up until bedtime that same evening to be exact. As soon as I heard the first of his lonely, pitiful wails, I snuck into the kitchen and brought Rusty into my bed with me where he snuggled quite comfortably under my covers. My parents found us cuddled together in the morning, with me sound asleep and Rusty wearing an expression that clearly announced that he had found a protector.

When I got to the kitchen later that morning, I was admonished for bringing the puppy into bed with me. I was reminded that Rusty was a hunting dog, not a pet to be spoiled. To this day, I swear I don't know what they were thinking! They actually thought they'd bring an adorable little puppy into the household and not expect me to spoil it? I chalk it up to a brief loss of their senses. In any case, my brother was quite proud that he had gotten a bird dog for his very own. He was telling all his friends about this great dog that was going to be his hunting partner and was the envy of all the other boys. Just as he was regaling all of his grand plans for his dog, I pedaled my bike around the corner with Rusty plopped in the basket dressed in doll clothes.

Rusty playing "Dress Up"

Needless to say, Rusty never did become a hunting dog. Once my father and brother admitted defeat in turning Rusty into a hunting dog, they too contributed to turning him into a spoiled pet. No one spoiled him more than me, though. And no matter what trouble he got into (and there was plenty of it), I would be right there to make excuses for him and protect him. He and I shared many great adventures through the years, playing make-believe and dress-up; something that my brother got sick over every time he witnessed it. Rusty lived out his years as my cherished childhood friend.

From an early age, I made it my mission to help save any wayward or injured animal that I could. I remember my father used to take me to a livestock auction on Saturday nights where they would sell any kind of animal imaginable. There were lots and lots of baby ducks there, I recall. "Daddy, what are they going to do with the ducks after they are sold?" My father looked at me with a sad expression and said, "Well, some of them will be used for breeding and producing eggs."

"And the others?" I asked.

"They get used for food, honey. Some people like to eat them."

I was abhorred. I couldn't believe that someone could actually want to eat the fuzzy, little critters I saw in front of me. The rest of the auction passed in a blur. During the week while driving down a road that we often used, I spotted a small farm with a pond. "Daddy, STOP!" I exclaimed. I made him pull into the driveway where I'd seen a huge flock of geese and ducks gathered around an old man who was feeding them. We asked him where he got all of them from, and he explained that he rescued some, and others were brought to him as adults after being raised in a family home from babies. They stayed there with him until they were ready to fly off and start families of their own.

The next weekend at the auction, I convinced Daddy to buy me some baby ducks to take home, raise and send to the old man with the duck sanctuary. Reluctantly, he agreed, thinking it would be a good experience for me, and quite frankly, knowing that I wasn't about to give up on the idea of rescuing my baby ducks. Truth be known, he was just as much a softy when it came to animals, and felt good about saving some of the ducks from slaughter.

The first clutch consisted of four flying mallards. They were only a couple of days old and still had to be fed every few hours on a special soft cereal diet the man at the feed store showed me how to mix. During the first few days of a ducks life, they are imprinted, or attached to the first thing they see move. That first movement they saw was from me, so from that time forward, they followed me as if I was their momma. It was really funny to see four little ducks waddling down the street after my bicycle!

My father and I built a sturdy pen in our backyard for the ducklings to live in, and watched them grow into mature, beautiful ducks then took them to the old man's sanctuary when it was time for them to go. Much to my mother's chagrin, we raised several more clutches after that, each time, letting them go when it was time for them to start their own families.

I learned a lot from raising the ducklings. Knowing that I was responsible for other living things instilled a sense of pride and commitment, along with a growing sense of self-confidence. I loved caring for the tiny ducklings and watching them blossom into beautiful adult birds. And even though it was hard letting them go, it felt good knowing that I saved a number of them from an uncertain future.

My grandfather was ultimately responsible for the next animal obsession. My mother, grandmother, grandfather and I were at a local farmer's market when they noticed me petting some baby bunnies a man had for sale. My grandfather asked my mother if he could buy me one. "Well, Dad," she said. "If you buy one for Kim, you have to buy one for Ricky, too." Seeing that there would be one bunny left all alone after buying one for me and one for my brother (my cousins were much older by this time, and my Mom knew they would not be interested in having a bunny of their own), my grandfather decided to buy all three of them.

We brought the bunnies home and elected my father to build them a hutch. He worked diligently and gave it his all. By the time he was done, the rabbits were living in style in their very own bunny-condo. My mother has always joked that my grandfather spent fifteen dollars on the rabbits, and my father spent a hundred and seventy-five building the cage! He got the raw end of the deal for sure, but as always, never complained.

We had the three rabbits for quite sometime, and fortunately, they all turned out to be females, so we weren't over-populated; at least, at first. While we were away on vacation, some of the kids in the neighborhood found a tame bunny all by itself and picked it up. They took it door to door, and couldn't find it's owner, so the kids that were taking care of our bunnies told them to put it in our hutch until they could figure out what to do. Within a few weeks, all three of our bunnies had babies, and so it continued until we had thirty-two rabbits! That was too many, even for me!

We gave away as many as we could, and separated the males and females to ensure that there would be no more babies, but still there were too many rabbits. The township had determined that it was too many as well, and cited us for having farm animals in a residential area. We had two weeks to get rid of all of the rabbits. I was broken hearted and remember crying as a neighbor's grandfather who owned a farm, came to collect every last one of them. I was quickly learning that caring for animals included great risk of getting your heart broke. That was one I was always willing to take, knowing that the rewards far surpassed any potential risk.

* * *

My grandfather was also the one who later introduced me to what would become a life-long love affair with horses. He used to take me riding at a local stable that offered pony rides on the weekends. From that first Saturday morning, I was hooked. My grandfather continued taking me for my weekly rides, and eventually passed the torch to my father when it appeared my hunger for riding would not be sated by weekend pony rides anymore. Dad took over feeding my passion in earnest. He was all for my interest in horses, since he saw it as a healthy hobby and figured that by having goals of becoming a better rider, I'd steer clear of the typical teen-age troubles. He found a stable that leased out ponies by the month so I could learn to ride on my own.

My parents, having realized that my thirst for knowledge about animals was not just a passing faze, did everything they could to foster my passion. They provided me with videos, books, and the "real" thing, allowing me to have many pets, which throughout the years included dogs, birds, turtles, ducks, rabbits, and finally; a horse.

Chapter Two

A close second to my love of animals has always been my love of the written word. As a pre-teen, I devoured books as if they were candy. It was always something so special to me, burying myself into a book. The idea that I could transport myself anywhere in the world, and be anyone I chose to be, simply by turning a page, was so appealing to me. I remember rushing to my next class in school, not so I'd have time to chat with my friends, but to finish the chapter I was reading of my latest horse novel. In addition, I always had the need to have pen and paper close at hand, lest I lose a passing idea for a story, or the stirrings of a budding poem.

Weaving the lives of beloved characters that I'd created in my mind into stories that brought them to life was always very exciting to me. What excited me even more was that I realized that if there was a story that I wish I could read about that I couldn't find, I could just write it myself!

I started my "mini-novels" in middle school. I actually was embarrassed to have anyone read them, being at such an impressionable and peer-pressured age. I did; however, show them to some very close friends, and to my surprise, they couldn't wait to read the next chapters. I'd get a kick out of them debating about what a character was going, or not going to do next. It was incentive for me to keep writing. And write I did! In a well-worn notebook, I took the advice of my writing teachers and I wrote everyday. I wrote descriptions of characters, I wrote ideas for the "great novel" I was going to pen one day, I wrote my deepest feelings without ambiguity, and I wrote creatively.

Poems have always come very naturally to me. I've always said that it is as if someone else were supplying the verses, I merely push the pen. Back then, I wrote about what I loved; horses mostly.

Poetry seemed the only way to adequately describe my intense love of this majestic creature.

I entered and placed in many writing contests, had my poetry published in school literature, and always scored straight A's in my English and writing classes. I simply loved meshing words with the appropriate emotions. Painting a mental picture by blending thoughts and feelings onto a blank sheet of paper gave me immense satisfaction, and was a great outlet for my emotions.

My family suggested that going to college for journalism might be a good career choice for me, not quite taking my riding as seriously as I did. I filed the idea in the back of my head and actually took a few courses needed in order to become a writer, thinking that writing was probably a good career choice. What I soon discovered, however, was that my poetry was something that was sacred to me. It was something I did for me, and only me. I didn't think that I could write something on demand without being able to show emotion and creativity. One month covering town hall meetings for a local newspaper confirmed my suspicions and ended my journalism career before it began.

As I suspected, my writing was not something I could force or coerce for any editor. It was special and pure; and it was mine. The characters in my stories were near and dear to me; and my poetry was my port in a storm. These were not things that I could compromise for anyone. I decided that my professional writing would have to take a back seat to my riding; at least for the time being.

I penned many poems throughout the years. I collected them in well-worn notebooks and file folders that overflowed with my hand-written notes and bits and pieces of ideas. I kept them and occasionally thumbed through them, enjoying looking back through my personal evolution. Whenever I shared my poetry with friends and family, I was urged to share them in the form of a published collection. Again, the idea sat in the back of my mind and was something that I planned to do sometime in the future. When this book began to take shape, I realized that my poetry chronicles my life from childhood through adulthood and paints a vivid picture with my raw, real emotions spilling out from each one. I also feel that I am not nearly the writer today as I was back then, at least not yet! It was important to me that I share some of what I was feeling back then in a way that I don't feel I can adequately describe today.

The following is a poetic walk through my own personal evolution.

This poem was one that I wrote in between classes in high school:

The Mighty Stallion
©1986 by Kimberly Carnevale

His clarion call rings out across his vast domain. With graceful, even strides, he gallops towards his opponent and screams again in vengeful hate. The fire in his eyes is burning deep in all its' fury He shortens his stride, his confidence brimming. His opponent is a worthy one—he to has fire in his eyes.

They rise to battle, teeth clenched and muscles tensed. As the furious battle rages on, the weaker of the two begins to fade. He no longer rushes and darts to avoid crushing blows and ravaging teeth. He knows he has lost and retreats once again to his solitary life.

The mighty stallion whistles in triumph. In every kingdom, there is but one king, and in every herd, there is but one leader—the mightiest stallion of them all!

From Winter To Spring
©1986 by Kimberly Carnevale

 As winter deals us it's icy wrath, I find myself longing for the coming of spring. In my mind's eye, I envision a whole new world awakening, pulling itself out of a fitful slumber.

 At times, I swear I feel it—and when I see my horses stop their play and raise their noses to taste the air, their gazes fixed on an unseen thing in the far distance; I realize they feel it too. They're remembering the warm spring breezes that whisper in their ears, encouraging them to race with the wind and feel it whip through their manes. They smell the flowers, so sweet to lie and roll in. They see the birds, busy in the preparation of their young ones to come. They taste the sweet, young grass and savor each mouthful, ever mindful of it's impending disappearance. But for now, it's time to don the winter blankets and break the ice in the water buckets.

 Once in a while, I'll tip-toe into the barn, just to make sure everyone's alright; and when I find them fast asleep, their ears twitching back and forth, I know they're dreaming of the whispering spring breezes calling them to play.

This poem was written after sharing a wonderfully exhilarating ride on one of my Thoroughbred racehorse friends:

Dancing With The Wind
©1998 by Kimberly Carnevale

Sitting in the starting gate,
waiting for the bell.
A thousand pounds of trembling flesh
released like a shotgun shell.

Soaring down the track,
he finds another gear.
Tucked up on his back,
I whisper in his ear,

"This is what you were born to do,
let your winged-hooves fly!"
Triumphing at the blinding speed
as the word goes whizzing by.

Never have I felt as one
with another soul.
Two hearts beat as one,
the earth comes undone—
tales of yesteryear foretold.

I drink in with wonder, his passion and drive;
thanking him for letting me share in his dance.
Caught by surprise at the tears in my eyes;
thanking the One up above for this chance.

Pounding down the stretch in the soft, deep, loam;
racing with the wind, his ancestors call him home.
I am but a witness to this ancient melody;
he hears songs of angels and sees things I can't see.

But he shares with me this romance
as we dance upon the wind,
and extends to me an invitation
to do it all again . . .

Dream On
© 1985 by Kimberly Carnevale

*I used to be a dreamer;
my goals I held so true.
I knew that when the chips were down,
my best would shine right through.*

*I worked all day and dreamed at night
of the things that were meant to be.
I never let the truth be known of the pain inside of me.*

*The dreams you hold in your heart
should be cherished and thought through.
You must reach inside and find the pride
that will make those dreams come true.*

*There will always be those who doubt you;
in their mind, nothing's real—
somehow they've forgotten
how dreams are supposed to feel.*

*At times you fight fatigue
and that never-ending pain . . .
just hold on 'till tomorrow—
and success will stop the rain.*

This was a poem that I wrote in high school when I imagined my filly, Precious Tika, (daughter of my mare, Lady Reign), growing up to be a harness racehorse:

First Start
©1986 by Kimberly Carnevale

*The field of eight fine horses
waiting for the bell.
The beating of the horses' hooves,
all are going well.*

*The bell goes off, the race begins;
the starter pulls away.
Three long years I've waited
for this very special day.*

*They make their way into the turn
building up more speed.
All are fighting really hard
to get into the lead.*

*The chestnut's coming 'round the turn,
the bay falls into line.
The black moves over to the real,
the others close in behind.*

*But here comes Precious Tika,
a maiden, yet a start.
Her heart will get her to the line—
her time's the best by far.*

*They sweep into the final turn
and Tika takes the lead.
What she lacks in experience
she makes up for with her speed.*

*Under the wire, it's Tika in front,
my head begins to spin.
My "little Tika," a racehorse at last,
just captured her very first win!*

This poem is an example of how I used my writing as an outlet for emotions that I had a hard time dealing with. It was written about my horse Sheeba, who died suddenly of an intestinal complication known as colic (I was about fourteen):

To Sheeba With Love
©1996 by Kimberly Carnevale

*I never dreamed that warm November day
would be your last.
I still can't believe it happened;
everything was going too fast.*

*I felt the sting of bitter tears,
I knew I faced my strongest fear.*

*You were in pain,
it was easy to see;
and you called for help—
your call was to ME.*

*I ran to you and told you
everything was going to be alright.
You seemed to understand
and you kept up your fight.*

*Your hooves were like weights
on your weakening feet.
Your head was hung low;
you were very, very weak.*

The vet had arrived,
but it was too late;
you were down on the straw
in your agonized state.

Your gentle eyes gazed into mine
as if to say, "It is my time."

You laid your head into my lap.
Then you were gone. Gone, just like that.

I cried for hours and days on end,
for I had just lost my most-loved friend.

This poem is very much like the last one, as it was written about our dog Rusty, who we got when I was eight years old. He died at age eleven.

My Dear, Old, Childhood Friend
©1995 by Kimberly Carnevale

*I'm holding onto our memories,
my dear, old, childhood friend.
I'm wishing for the happy times
we thought would never end.*

*I remember when I was just a little girl,
and you were just a pup.
I remember your never-ending patience,
even when I dressed you up!*

*I recall the changing seasons,
each one bringing something new.
No matter what the weather,
I knew I could always count on you.*

*You didn't use words to express yourself,
yet you were as clear as you could be.
Those big, brown eyes; so sweet and wise
used to speak to me.*

*You were my shoulder to cry on
and you always lent your ear.
Your faithfulness was undaunted
and your love for me was clear.*

But before I knew what happened,
we both were all grown up.
I was no longer a little girl
and you were no longer a pup.

One day I was startled to find
that you had suddenly grown old.
In your eyes I saw no youngster,
but a very contented soul.

You faced with grace and dignity
the end you knew to come.
I think you somehow realized
that Fate had finally won.

The inevitable was upon us
and I whispered in your ear.
I said, "I love you," softly
and for the last time, held you near.

Your time came all too soon
and we were forced to say, "good-bye."
You drew in your last breath
and the pain faded from your eyes.

I don't know if my broken heart
will ever truly mend,
but I will always save a very special place
for my dear, old, childhood friend.

There were many times when a poem would jump into my head unexpectedly and completely finished. This one popped into my head and out onto paper within five minutes. We were on the way to my grandmother's funeral. I wrote it down on the way to the car, and it was read at the service in tribute:

Going Home
©1998 by Kimberly Carnevale

Hear the voices
calling out to you.
Open the door
and go right through.

Angels to show you
Heaven's helm.
Your soul commended
to His great realm.

Don't worry about loved ones
you're leaving behind—
they'll join you one day
when it is their time.

Fear not, my loved one—
you are not alone;
He is waiting for you—
you are going home.

This was another poem that I woke up with in the middle of the night. It is quite dark, and scary actually; yet gives an adequate description of a nightmare that I'd had (I think this was a night that I had watched a scary movie before bed!):

Again . . .
©1997 by Kimberly Carnevale

Gloomy shadows
cast upon a cold, forgotten past.

Shards of a broken heart
lie among the rubble
of young girl's dreams.

A sorrowful face
streaked by flaming tears of anger
illuminate the depths
of this final resting place.

Sinister remains
of a past execution—
soon to be forgotten
in the icy winds of Time.

Silence will befall the stillness—
shattered only by the faint beating of a broken heart.

Refusal to die
is a lasting desire to live.
Yet the desire to live
is smoldered by an unforgiving past;
one to which there are many beginnings—
one to which there is only one end . . .

Sometimes I wrote to express my feelings, but sometimes I wrote simply to write. My creative writing teacher in ninth grade gave me an assignment to set a timer for five minutes and write whatever came to mind without thinking about it. This was the result:

Emotionless beyond compare. Human fallacy declares the carelessness that hides behind the normalcy of compassion.

Look towards the sun—it is there you shall find the conclusion to the final destination. Silence—ever present through trees set afire by the scorching sun of mid-August. The sunlight finally splashes down upon a lonely forest floor; finding its final destination upon a flourishing dream that has no end.

A fiery sunset streaks across a sleepy sky to envision its everlasting radiance—spectacular radiance that illuminates a world of gloom and hatred. A symphony of proud, everlasting love—lasting only for a moment; innocence long since forgotten . . .

There were poems I wrote about things that were going on in my own life, others depicted events in my friends' lives, some were derived from bits of other people's conversations that I would hear throughout my day, still others were simply made up from my imagination:

Dream World
©1986 by Kimberly Carnevale

> *Void of all the darkness*
> *and danger out of sight;*
> *I slip into my dream world*
> *each and every night.*
>
> *I wander into silence*
> *and emptiness beyond.*
> *The peacefulness is soothing—*
> *all my worries, gone.*
>
> *I'm alone, but not forsaken,*
> *for I'm in complete control.*
> *I can come back anytime I wish,*
> *or finish playing out my role.*
>
> *I can go higher than the mountains,*
> *or deeper than the seas.*
> *There are no limitations*
> *to where my dreams can carry me.*
>
> *I can relive special memories*
> *from he present or the past.*
> *I don't worry about the future*
> *because my troubles just can't last.*

*But my favorite part of dreaming
is the ability to see,
all the different places
my mind can carry me.*

*Misty corners of darkness
are sure to give a fright,
but once I'm in my dream world,
everything's alright.*

Storm-Crossed Lovers
© by Kimberly Carnevale

*The sea is rough and stormy,
and I can't yet see the sun.
Rising on a swell of life,
I see what's said and done.*

*As the next swell rises to meet the first
and sends me on my way,
I see the glimmer of light and hold the hope
of the dawn of a brighter day.*

*A day when the storm cloud passes
and releases it's hold on me—
a day when sunlight splashes
and shines its warmth from Thee.*

*And shine it will on both of us,
lost among our storm-crossed paths!
To dwell in peace and harmony,
bathed in the love that Heaven's cast.*

Just Reach Out
©1992 by Kimberly Carnevale

The road ahead may seem dark and gloomy;
you think the hell won't ever end.
When the going gets too tough
and you think you've had enough;
just reach out—you've got a friend.

Everyone needs a friend,
no matter how strong they are.
So if you ever need me,
just reach out—I won't ever be too far.

I may not feel your pain;
not to say I don't understand.
If you need someone to help you,
just reach out—I'll be there to lend a hand.

The courage you have inside you
will see you through each day.
But if that courage ever fails you,
just reach out—I'll help you find the way.

*Don't ever feel alone,
you've got many loved ones behind you.
But if you ever feel doubt,
just reach out—I'll be right there to remind you.*

*If you need a shoulder to cry on,
or a sympathetic ear;
just reach out—I'm a friend,
that's exactly why I'm here.*

*Everyday you'll grow stronger
and before you know it you'll be on track.
When that time comes;
just reach out—I'll be the first one to welcome you back.*

Laying Love To Rest
©1990 by Kimberly Carnevale

I remember a time,
not so long ago;
a loving arm around me
a promise to not let go.

Dancing to a soothing melody
our bodies sway in bliss.
I remember well your sweet request—
you asked me for a kiss.

Love grew stronger
and I thought I'd found
the one to share my life.
As Fate would have it
one special night,
you asked me to be your wife.

Turn the page,
another chapter has begun—
the man that once adored me
has started to run.

*A love that once desired me
has now pushed me away.
The soul I used to understand
gets stranger everyday.*

*I wonder what I did,
or what I've left undone.
Is it just me,
or has he found someone?*

*No longer does he look at me
as if I hung the moon—
dispassionate expressions
now replace his former swoon.*

*Behind the door of my heart,
it struggles to beat alone—
bravely facing pain,
it flutters its' old, familiar drone.*

*Someone sent it flowers today,
with a pretty card inside—
"Condolences in this difficult time;
so sorry Love has died."*

Thank You
©1995 by Kimberly Carnevale

> *Thank you...*
> *...for giving me a shoulder to lean on,*
> *an ear to complain to*
> *and a heart to understand.*
>
> *Thank you...*
> *...for giving me advice,*
> *sharing my pain*
> *and lending a helping hand.*
>
> *Sorry...*
> *...if I seem sort of distant and far away;*
> *struck be hind the clouds,*
> *hidden on a rainy day.*
>
> *Please be patient...*
> *...because soon the storm will pass*
> *and let my heart go free.*
> *I'll revel in the sun*
> *and introduce you to the REAL me.*

When I Look Into Your Eyes
©1996 by Kimberly Carnevale

When I look into your eyes
I see all the things I've dreamed of
and then I realize
This is what was meant to be
two hearts—entwined forever
bound by destiny.

You saved my heart from drowning
in a pool of broken dreams.
and now you've given me the strength
to find out just what true love means.

When I looked into my soul
to find the one true love I needed,
it was you who made me whole.

Forever is our journey's end,
each step we take is ours;
so now I give to you my gifts of love—
the moon, the sky, the stars . . .

You Ask Me IF I Love You
©1998 by Kimberly Carnevale

*You ask me if I love you
I can't think of what to say.
What I feel inside for you
grows stronger every day.*

*Mere words cannot express
the magic of your touch
stirring things inside of me—
wanting you so much*

*Sometimes I secretly study
the outline of your face.
I fall into your loving eyes
and ache for your embrace.*

*I think of all the dreams we'll share
when tomorrow dawns.
Walking hand in hand forever
all our worries—gone.*

*I can't say when it happened—
How? I haven't got a clue.
I only know for certain
that yes, Dear—I do love you.*

Eighteen Wheels
©1998 By Kimberly Carnevale

While lines in between us
as she carries him away.
He says he loves me dearly—
yet not enough to stay.

Eighteen Wheels sings to him softly,
caressing his childhood fantasy.
Life on the road; precious cargo to load—
there's no room left for me.

There's no way to compete
with a mistress who he dresses up in chrome.
she not only provides him a way of life;
she offers him a home.

I'm merely just a rest stop—
his mistress I can't fight.
Eighteen Wheels carries him away again
deep into the night.

A formidable opponent,
I guess she's finally won.
It's clear just where his heart lies now—
there's no more to be done.

Take care of him, Eighteen Wheels,
for out of all the things you haul,
that man guiding you down the highway
is the most precious cargo of all . . .

Midnight Fright
©1986 by Kimberly Carnevale

*In the darkness of night he whispers
an old, forgotten prayer.
From the pages of time he reaches out
and lures you to his lair.*

*The road so dark and gloomy;
once traveled, not explored.
Just a one way ticket, no turning back;
to the end it is you're lured.*

*The challenge of a lifetime
is right there at your feet.
but win or lost he'll take you;
this demon can't be beat.*

*You gave into this viper;
a grave and bold mistake.
You should have just ignored him—
indifference would ensure your escape.*

*In his eyes burns a fire
that reaches deep inside your soul.
He has no limitations;
your capture is his goal.*

*But a brand new day is dawning
and you find that you're alright.
It was pure imagination,
and a little midnight fright!*

Don't Stop Doing What You Do To Me
©1998 by Kimberly Carnevale

Bringing down a wall
I fought so hard to build;
traipsing through resolve
with your iron will.

Sweetly spoken words
falling off your tongue
whisper soft caresses
warm me like the sun.

Your eyes, they see right through me—
light green windows to your soul.
You stepped inside despite my pride
so that love could take control.

Riding on a wave of passion,
surfing on the swells—
Our two hearts rise and fall
to meet where true love dwells.

*Keeping with tradition
two hearts beating side by side;
dancing to an ancient song
coming from inside.*

*Loving you, loving me; it's what was meant to be.
Holding on into the night—
don't stop doing what you do to me.*

A Love For All Time
©1999 by Kimberly Carnevale

    Un deniable proof looks me in the eye;
    evidence of a hidden love—
    once again he's lied.

    How many times I told myself
    to simply walk away.
    Yet despite the pain and misery;
    still, I chose to stay.

    Did I set myself up for a fall
    or hold onto a dying dream?
    Funny how things work out—
    people aren't always what they seem.

    I thought that we could work it out—
    this man I loved so dear.
    Strange; I hurt so badly,
    yet can no longer shed a single tear.

    Wasn't so long ago,
    we shared so many dreams.
    Today he's off in someone else's world
    longing for something else, it seems.

That faraway look has concerned me;
it's been there for a while.
I always made excuses;
he'd cover it with a smile.

We've had our share of problems;
everyone has a few.
I thought that we could conquer them—
I thought we'd make it through.

No longer do we share kisses
in the warm, coastal sand.
We no longer hold each other—
he won't even hold my hand.

So how can I compete
with this distance he's put between our hearts,
and how can I forget the betrayal that's tearing me apart?

To heal my broken heart,
I must let go of the past;
no more broken promises
from a man who couldn't last.

As I try to picture my future, it's difficult to see
a life without the one I loved
and at one time, still loved me.

Even though he's hurt me,
despite the tears I've cried;
a part of me still loves him—
a part that just won't die.

*Cherished memories filter though
like sunlight through the rain.
I can't help but think
off all the special times
I long to live again.*

*Trembling legs below me,
please don't let me fall.
Almighty God above me,
hear my desperate call.*

*Let me find the strength
I once felt inside my heart.
Give to me the confidence
to make a whole new start.*

*Let me find a love
that once, I thought I'd found.
Let me find the man
who'll never let me down.*

*I need someone to comfort me;
one who'll hold me when I cry.
I need someone to give me answers
when I'm left to wonder, "Why?"*

*I need to see in his eyes
a love that mirrors mine.
I need to find a man
who'll love me for all time.*

Chapter Three

People have often asked me how a kid growing up just outside of Trenton, New Jersey gets so involved in animals, and much more surprising, to compete in equestrian events. It wasn't as if my family was involved, or even interested in horses. Looking back now, I see that it was inevitable. It was something that I was born to do. Neither financial nor geographical limitations could dissuade me from learning all I possibly could about my passion.

An innate rider, I was a student of the horse. Every time I was astride an equine friend, I set out to see just how close I could get to him. I studied their language, their movements, their emotions; I needed to understand them and wanted them to understand me. They were my friends, and I wanted them to consider me as such. It was a gift. A treasured gift handed down from God that gave me the desire and ability to innately connect with all things animal. Dr. Doolittle? I don't think so—more like an honorary membership of an animal alliance that I was proud to claim membership.

My obsession with horses was exactly that—an obsession. It definitely helped that I had very understanding parents who recognized my dream and did all they could to help my riding ambition. Fortunately for me, Dad loved horses as well. He'd always wanted to ride as a boy, but he'd grown up in a single-parent home during the Great Depression and there was no way for him to realize his boy-hood dream. In some ways, I believe he lived out his unrequited dreams through me.

My father diligently drove me to the stables each day after school and on weekends, and I think he enjoyed it almost as much as I did. When I outgrew my pony, he and my mom worked very hard at scraping up the money to buy me my first horse. Dad would help me groom and saddle my horse and both my parents would enjoy watching me ride, although Mom always got nervous watching me jump.

    I got my first horse when I was about nine years old. She was purchased through a dealer that had advertised her in the newspaper. We needed a place to keep her, and really hit it off with the dealer named Bob, so we decided to board her at his facility. Bob Carroll voluntarily took on the job of turning me into a real horsewoman. He was an older man who had lots of horses and a lifetime of experience. He didn't ride himself anymore because of a bad back, but he gave me impromptu instruction, if you can call it that, from the ground and left me to figure out most of it myself. He believed that learning came from doing, and was very tough on me, instilling that if something was worth doing, it was worth doing right. He showed me how to clean stalls properly, maintain a stable, groom a horse until it looked like it was going to Sunday school, taught me about the horse industry from the point of view of a dealer, and gave me the opportunity to ride just about everything you could imagine from huge Thoroughbreds, to small ponies, to an occasional donkey! We would accompany him weekly to various horse sales, and he would have me ride the prospects he was considering that day. There were always about ten to fifteen horses in his stable at any one time, and once they came home, Bob would have me work with those that needed a little extra fine tuning. These experiences were invaluable because in riding all sorts of different types of horses, I encountered different problems that he helped me work out and solve. As my riding improved, Bob would buy greener horses and have me work with them until they were sold for a considerable profit. My cut would be applied to my horse's monthly board, and eventually, I began earning above and beyond board and started to stash away a little extra cash that was used for extras such as treats, new brushes, and such.

    When I was about fourteen-years old, my father purchased Lady Reign, a two-year old Standardbred mare for me to train. She was bred to be a racehorse, but was temporarily laid up due to a tendon strain. We planned to return her to the racetrack after her layoff, but I took her training to an entirely different plateau.

Standardbreds are notorious in the harness racing industry, pulling carts called sulkies, and at that time, were not considered riding prospects.

While I tended to Lady Reign's injury, I became acutely aware of her many attributes that made me believe that she would make a great riding horse. By that time, Bob had retired from the horse business and moved to Florida, and the hundred-acre farm was taken over by Standardbred racehorse trainers. Many professional horsemen that had racehorses stabled at the farm scoffed at my "hair-brained" scheme and reminded me of the age-old belief that Standardbreds were just for racing. The way I figured it, if it had four legs, a mane and a tail, I'd ride it!

We started off with long, slow walks, ever mindful of her still-rehabilitating injury. Having already been trained to harness, bit and bridle, most of my work was done as far as "breaking" her, or getting her used to a rider on her back. As her leg got stronger, I incorporated circles, serpentines, and other patterns into her daily rides in order to help teach her how to "collect" herself. Collection, a term used in the equestrian world to describe the point where a horse lifts it's front end and pushes it's weight rearward, engaging the "engine" or hind end in order to be lighter and more responsive in the rider's hands. When a horse is collected, or engaged, its gaits are smoother, more consistent, and more powerful. It takes a long time to teach collection, because you are not just teaching a skill, you are building muscles that are required in order to perform the skill fluently and consistently.

Spending the amount of time it took to teach Lady Reign collection also gave me the opportunity to fall in love with her funny, often quirky, but always gentle, loving disposition. Needless to say, Lady Reign never did make it back to the racetrack! Instead our time was spent on long trail rides, training for weekend horseshows, and eventually, doing demonstrations on behalf of her breed at fairs, racetracks, and other equestrian events all over the East coast. Lady Reign took me to three national championships, earning Champion two years out and Reserve Champion in her last and final attempt at the tender age of eighteen! We set out and succeeded in shattering the archaic myth and proved without a doubt that Standardbreds are NOT just for racing anymore!

When I started competing, my father eagerly adopted the status of "Horseshow Dad," a title that is worn as a badge of honor by parents of children in the horseshow world. Horseshow parents are a hearty bunch. Through half-opened eyes, they wordlessly arise at ungodly early hours of the day to shuttle their child to horseshow after horseshow. Their job is one that epitomizes the art of multi-tasking. They are there to help calm nerves, smooth out wrinkles in hunt coats, wipe slobber from horses' lips, pick hooves, return to trailer for forgotten items, remove ketchup stains from white breeches apply a last-minute dust and shine to a child's boots and horses' coat, single-handedly create a cheering section, await with cool/warm drinks at the end of each class, congratulate/console on the outcome of the day's events, help to pack up and load equipment, horse, and said child onto the trailer and into the car (respectively), and back home again, only to start making arrangements for the following weekend's show!

Family functions were planned around horse activities, and after-school events took a back seat to horse shows. To say I was obsessed with my riding was an understatement! I felt a tremendous need to learn and strive to be the best horsewoman I could possibly be. I poured over every book and article I could about horses. I studied their behaviors, and the behaviors of other animals as well. I spent hours absorbed in countless episodes of educational animal programs broadcast on television. I learned about dogs, horses, birds, and cats; in short, I devoured any and all information of everything animal.

Since we couldn't afford a riding instructor for me, I was forced to take on my equestrian education on my own. Bob's "ride by the seat of your pants" method of teaching notwithstanding, I literally learned how to ride by reading books and magazines. I would read an article, take pages upon pages of notes, and practice what I'd learned the next time I rode. I would have Dad videotape me riding so that I could see what I was doing wrong and go back to my books to learn how to fix it. I would continue this self-teaching throughout most of my career.

Once I'd gotten the taste of showing and competing, I was hooked. I loved it; I craved it. When I found that people do it for a living, I had my career choice. I was going to ride, train and compete horses for a living. I would have my own stables, my own clients, and my own show horses. I would work really hard, learn everything I could so that I could tackle my ultimate goal; I was going to ride on the United States Equestrian Team. I never was one to think small.

Even though my parents supported me unendingly, they also tried to tone down my ambition of riding on the Team. Concerned that I was heading for a great let down, they gently tried to persuade me to re-vamp my visions of Olympic Gold. They had very good points; we didn't have the money for a coach, I didn't have the caliber of horse needed for that level of competition, or the financial backing to get me to the pinnacle of my dreams. Undaunted, I continued to dream and work towards my goal. As a matter of fact, the more people that told me I couldn't do it, the more determined I became to prove them wrong.

By age sixteen, I was exercising and grooming the Standardbred racehorses that were stabled at the farm in exchange for board for my own horse. Everyday after school, I would do my homework, then change into my barn clothes to muck stalls and exercise horses in exchange for my own horse's upkeep. The owner of the stable, seeing how keen I was to learn, exposed me to as many learning experiences as he could, always teaching and sharing with me the knowledge that he'd accumulated over a life-time with horses. Summers were spent following the farriers and veterinarians on their rounds, always asking questions and trying new skills.

While the work was physically very hard, it was also lots of fun! I would often spend the night at my friend, Kim's house. We both boarded our horses at the farm and had been friends for most of our lives. It was about three miles from her house to the farm and we would ride our dirt bikes over to the barn. We met up with other friends from the barn and after all the chores were done, we always found time for a water fight or bareback trail ride. On special race days, we'd accompany the owner to the racetrack with one of the stable's horses to watch it race. It was very exciting, and we considered it quite a privilege to harness the horse and lead it to the post parade, hopefully get our photo taken in the winner's circle, and take the horse back to the barn for it's bath and cool down. It was in those early days that I'd established a solid foundation to launch my budding career as a professional horsewoman.

While not interested in following the Standardbred racing circuit long term, the skills that I was learning were invaluable. Even though I was working very hard with the racehorses, I still made time for horseshows. I spent long hours preparing my horse, Lady Reign, for each show, trying my best and coming home a winner in my heart, no matter what ribbon I'd earned. I loved it. The competition drove me to excel and strive to be my best, not only with my riding, but also with my relationship with my horse. It was as if the judges were telling me, "Okay, let's see how close you can get to communicating effectively with your horse." It was a challenge I couldn't pass up.

I skipped both my junior and senior proms because of horseshows. I ate, slept, and breathed horses! When I was seventeen, I had learned how to ride the Thoroughbred racehorses that had moved into one of our barns, and discovered the true meaning of "horse power." By the time I graduated high school, I was earning decent money training race and show horses for clientele, but only part-time. I rode and trained in the evenings and competed on weekends, as my parents insisted that it would be best for me to have a "real job," one with benefits and a 401k, so that I could fall back on it should the "horse thing" not work out.

Although my parents were unarguably my greatest fans, they knew well the vacillating aspects of the horse industry. There are many shady deals, and even shadier characters in the horse business. They knew it was a hard way to earn a living, especially for a girl, and didn't want to see me get hurt, physically or financially. We had many discussions about my wanting to train horses full-time; still, I respected their advice and saw merit in their argument. I begrudgingly agreed to maintain my horses as a hobby and work around the barriers of my day job in order to train for the U.S.E.T.

Me and my Mom and Dad at a horseshow

Chapter Four

If I was going to work a job that didn't include horses, it was going to have to be an interesting job. I utilized my skills that I'd learned following the equine veterinarians on their rounds to land a job as a veterinary technician in a small animal hospital. The job fulfilled me, and I was good at it, unfortunately, it didn't pay enough to cover my bills. Over the next couple of years, I tried going to two other practices, but raises were few and far between, and I just couldn't make financial ends meet. My brother's boss informed me of an opening in our local Sheriff's Department, working as a clerk in the foreclosure department. It sounded interesting enough and I took it, biding my time, I knew, until the day came when I would summon up enough courage to strike out in the horse world full time.

Working in the Sheriff's Department proved a lot more interesting than I originally anticipated it to be. My job entailed preparing foreclosed properties for weekly Sheriff's sale, and assisting in the sales themselves. It was work that was always changing and I found myself actually enjoying it.

Spending time in the courthouse exposed me to the job of Sheriff's Officer. I got friendly with some of the officers, and often found myself wishing I were going with them on their rounds. What really hooked me though, was meeting the drug and bomb dogs in the canine unit. The canine officers knew how much I loved animals, so they would be sure that they visited my office on their daily rounds. As I'd always done in the stables, I asked countless questions about their training and handling procedures. I was fascinated and wanted to learn more.

About the same time that my interest in the canine unit peaked, a timid female German Shepard was recruited for training. The sergeant in charge of the unit was having difficulties with her because she did not respond well to men. Knowing about my love of animals and desire to learn more about the canine unit, he would bring her into my office and allow me to spend some time with her, trying to get her more comfortable in a strange environment. In an offhanded discussion, I'd mentioned that I would love to be able to trade in my desk job for an official assignment on the canine unit. I was told about the next written test for Sheriff's Officer that was to be given, and signed up. I scored a very respectable ninety-eight percent on my written test, and was awaiting notice about my academy assignment.

I was pretty content at that point in that the job that I was settling for was actually panning out to be something that I was really interested in. I still continued with the horses on the weekends, though, and a big part of me still wished that I were at the barn instead of the courthouse. My parents insisted that I was doing the right thing, though, because I had a steady job that paid well, had great county benefits and a pretty bright future as Sheriff's Officer. I kept telling myself that, too. After all, I liked what I was doing and was excited about working with the canine unit, I should be happy, right? I knew I should be, but there was no denying the constant nagging that my heart yearned to be somewhere else. Weekend shows weren't enough anymore. I pushed down the great, big lump of regret that rose in my throat every time the horseshow circuit moved away from home during the week and I longed to be going with it. Still, I was doing the right thing; at least that was what my Dad kept telling me.

In 1994, my Dad taught me the biggest lesson of my life, and showed me how wrong he'd been. He taught me that whatever you strive for in life, you have to hold onto with every ounce of courage and tenacity you possess. You have to dare to dream, and even more importantly, strive for excellence in pursuing your dreams; even if others tell you it's impossible. If he were here today, I believe he'd say something like, "Never let anyone stand in your way of attaining your heart's desire." He's not here to tell me that, though, because on November 3, 1994, he died suddenly of a massive heart attack.

For close to thirty years, my father worked a postal job that he hated; truly hated, in order to earn a good living and support his family. I remember him saying countless times, "If I had it to do all over again, I'd have paid closer attention in school and learned a trade I really enjoyed." He hated going to work, every single day, right up until his retirement. He convinced my mother to retire from her job a couple of years later because they planned to take a trip they'd talked about for years, traveling by train across the country to visit some relatives. They had made all the arrangements and were very excited about finally doing something they'd dreamed of all those years, but they never got to do it. He died, and all his unfulfilled dreams died with him. He worked all those years at a job he hated, only to die before he got to do what he really wanted to do; it all seemed so very sad to me.

I was absolutely devastated by my father's death. For weeks, I was inconsolable; I stopped being able to function properly. I was even hospitalized at one point, on the verge of a nervous breakdown. I could not sleep, sometimes for days at a time, because night terrors had taken control of my grief-stricken mind. I was unable to eat, and was tube-fed for a week. Upon release from the hospital, I went into grief counseling, trying desperately to learn how to cope with the loss of my beloved father.

My father's death was traumatic in itself, yet it brought out other disturbing issues that had remained carefully hidden beneath layers of denial and years of guilt. Layers so thick, that even to this day, it is hard for me to talk about. The difficulty I have facing what happened to me nearly prevented me from sharing this next piece of my life in this book, however, in careful introspection, and with advice from close family and friends, I felt the need to share everything so that I may correctly portray the insight of what it is to overcome life's more complicated challenges.

The night terrors, we later learned were a result of my mind's inability to accept that I no longer had my father's protection. His protection was vital to me, not so much in the physical sense, but in that when I was twelve I was involved in an attempted kidnapping, and when I was fourteen, I was sexually assaulted by my doctor during my very first gynecological exam. Subconsciously, I saw my father as a shield that warded off all future danger and even provided me with an escape from sorting through my emotional scars. These issues were never truly dealt with on my part, as I saw how much it upset those around me to deal with my pain, and so I used that as a convenient excuse to shut it away, dooming it to eternity harbored with the fear, guilt and shame that the incidents produced.

Caught up in a flood of walled up emotions, my troubled mind tried desperately to swim through the river of despair, only to be swept away by the current of repression. It took everything I had to bring out these issues in therapy, but I knew the only way to be rid of them was to talk about them and finally take back the power they had over me. Thinking back now, I look at repressed feelings like a wound that is trying to heal. It may hurt to initially clean a cut, but if you don't get out all the germs, they will fester until the wound becomes infected. However, if you take a deep breath, face all the pain at once and get rid of the germs, the wound will heal and that's the end of it. Such was the case with my repressed guilt and fear from the abduction and assault. It was very painful, but once I rid myself of them, I was able to carry on, knowing that those things were things that happened to me, not because of me. All in all, my father's death left me feeling scared, exposed and very uncertain of my future.

Nothing made sense to me anymore. I felt the need to "shake things up." From behind my desk at the Sheriff's Department, I would spend countless hours daydreaming about quitting my job and making my passion of training horses a full-time endeavor. Then one day, I stopped dreaming and did it. It was the best decision of my life.

Chapter Five

I finally realized my dream of making horses a full-time job. It was hard leaving the friends that I'd made in the Sheriff's Office, but I knew I needed to do it, nonetheless. The constant internal nagging that I'd endured during the two and a half years I'd spent at the Sheriff's Department disappeared all at once, and even though striking out on my own was a scary endeavor, I knew that I was doing the right thing.

I had the good fortune of boarding my horses at a facility in which the management was very flexible. The owner's daughter was a good friend of mine, as she and I had trained and competed together for quite a while. She convinced her father to allow me to sublet a section of stalls in which to stable my clients' horses. Since I'd already had a successful part-time following there, it didn't take long for word-of-mouth advertising to fill up the rest of my stalls. I was in business! I took in show and racehorses on an individual contract basis.

Eager to build a full-time following, I took every job I could, riding every type of horse I could. I rode horses getting ready to go up for sale that needed a fine-tuning, I rode "rouges" that needed attitudinal adjustments, and at dawn's first light, I made a stop at nearby Philadelphia Park Racetrack and I exercised thoroughbred racehorses, marveling at the speed and power of the magnificent animal beneath me. If it had four legs, a mane and a tail, I'd ride it!

My forte was the babies, two and three year-old youngsters who had yet to learn the basics of being handled and ridden. These wide-eyed, spindly-legged creatures would come to me barely having been taught to lead and follow a human being. It was my job to teach them trust and respect and turn them into well-behaved equine citizens.

The early days of a young horse's career are the most crucial. Lessons, both good and bad, learned at this stage last a lifetime. Working with young horses can be a very difficult, yet rewarding endeavor. It can be very dangerous, as young horses are known to be fractious and very unpredictable. However, molding an uncooperative colt into a highly trained athlete can make all the hardships worthwhile. It also taught me unending patience and perseverance, something that would prove to be invaluable to me in the years to come.

I would often revel in my decision to train horses full-time. I was greeted by the nickering of horses and the sweet smell of hay, horses, and leather every morning. Every afternoon I was *paid* to ride, and every evening, I went home physically tired and deliriously happy looking forward to yet another day of "work."

Brandy

One of the perks from working at the barn was that I was able to bring my dog, Brandy, to work with me. Brandy was a sweet, beautiful, shorthaired Collie that I had rescued a couple of years before. She had been a frightened, abandoned stray when I found her. So frightened, that it took me a half-hour and a piece of meat to lure her close enough to get a hold of her. It took several months of loving care to earn her trust, but it was well worth it! Brandy was a great dog. She had a loving, intuitive nature that simply made you fall helplessly, hopelessly in love with her. And I did, big time. She was my constant companion. Brandy went to work with me each day, was welcome at the local feed store (they usually had a special treat saved for her), went to all my competitions to cheer me on, and snuggled up with me each night. She had made such an impact of me that I knew that for the rest of my life, I would share my home with a Collie.

There was one dog I'd never imagined sharing my home with. His name was Dewey, and he was a giant! Dewey was a St. Bernard/German Shepard mix who had plenty of love to give, but no one to give it to. His was a life of strife and depravity. He belonged to the caretaker of the farm where I boarded my horses. Unfortunately, the caretaker didn't take very good care of him. Dewey had spent the entire eighteen months of his life tethered by a ten-foot chain to the porch of a mobile trailer that was his home. He had never been to a veterinarian, so he wasn't neutered, or even inoculated. His ears were raw and bleeding from the constant barrage of flies that plagued him day after day, and his coat was sparse and missing in some places from allergic reactions to innumerable fleabites.

Oftentimes when I was alone at the barn, I would sneak over to where Dewey was tied and apply medication to his wounds and give him cans of dog food and fresh, cool water. He and I became fast friends, and I ached to be able to do more for him.

One afternoon, I was grooming one of my show horses when I overheard the farm's owner say that he'd be taking Dewey later that day to have him put to sleep. I hurried over to him and asked what was going on. Dewey's owner had been arrested and apparently wasn't getting out of jail anytime in the near future. Dewey was without a home and there was no one left to care for him. The farm management believed it would be kinder to have the dog humanely destroyed rather than him having to wait out the time in the pound for an adoption that would never happen. We all knew the eighty-five pound, untrained dog was not a good candidate for adoption, but it seemed so unfair. It wasn't his fault he wasn't taught manners, and he was still a baby! A big baby, for sure, but he deserved better.

Dewey

Before I could stop the words from tumbling from my lips, I'd told the farm owner I would take him. Just like that, I was the owner of an over-grown, over-zealous, untrained pup named Dewey. My plan was to take him home, put some training into him, and make him adoptable. It worked. I took him home, put some training into him, and I adopted him. I had no idea that four years later, he'd return the favor.

Dewey fit right into our family. He and Brandy got along great, and he actually learned a lot from her. Brandy was an extremely obedient dog; she had to be in order to be safe around the horses. She was a great role model for Dewey, and was a great asset in his training. From learning house-training to walking on a leash, and finally off-leash training, Brandy set an example for Dewey and made life a whole lot easier for me! I applied many of the training skills I'd learned while watching the canine unit at the Sheriff's department and soon Brandy and I had turned Dewey into a well-behaved canine citizen. Now I had the company of both my dogs at work!

Other boarders and their guests had known Dewey prior to his "transformation," and were very impressed by his training. Before I knew it, I had several requests for training pet dogs! Training dogs was second nature, and I was still pretty much desperate to earn enough money to keep my budding business afloat, so I accepted the requests. What I soon discovered was that I really wasn't training the dogs as much as I was training the owners to communicate more effectively with their canine friends.

In teaching my methods to others, I'd learned something very valuable. I'd never really thought about training animals before. It just came naturally; I didn't think about it, I just did it. By breaking down the lessons I used in my training, I was able to see for myself exactly why it worked. It worked because I was communicating with the animal in its' language, not mine. In my years of studying animal behavior, I discovered that animals use a highly developed mode of communication that can be duplicated and reproduced. Animal communication can be likened to sign language. Sign language is not audible, yet still perfectly clear to those who know it.

We all know sign language to a certain extent. If I were to wave to you while approaching, you would know I was saying, "hello." If I were to put my index finger over my pursed lips, you'd know I was saying, "quiet," and so on. Animals relate in this way as well, only their signals are a bit different. They use body language to communicate with one another; and with us, only most of us try to communicate to an animal in our words instead of gestures that they innately understand.

For example, one of my earliest equine lessons that I'd learned was that when a horse laid his ears flat back and flared his nostrils it meant that he wasn't happy about something and may be getting ready to lash out. I also learned that by walking up to a horse just behind it's shoulder, I could make him move forward, and by shifting my position slightly ahead of the shoulder, the horse would stop. Additionally, if I approached a submissive horse, lowered my heard and turned to walk away, the horse would follow. These are all bits of the language that horses use amongst themselves. When it comes to training any type of animal, it's up to us to pay close attention in order to interpret and utilize their body language. By studying an animal's language and learning to communicate with it on this very primal level, we can expect to be much more successful in our training endeavors.

From my earliest memories, I'd spent endless hours watching animals interact with one another. I'd sit out in the turnout field, observing how the horses exhibited their excitement, joy, fear, and anger. I watched them resolve their issues and marveled how a seemingly violent situation could be resolved in seconds by a simple shift of position or modification of expression.

The same held true when I watched dogs interacting. They relate in the same, wordless, yet highly commutative way. I watched my dogs as they played with the other dogs at the farm. There was a pecking order that they all observed and respected. If two dogs tried to be "alpha" or lead dog, there would be a brief confrontation, made up of dominate gestures meaning, "Don't mess with me, I'm bigger and stronger than you!" Sometimes younger and less socialized dogs would try and pass the alpha dog, a social "don't" in the animal kingdom. The alpha would quickly seize the offending animal in what looked like a brutal, malicious attack; grabbing the scruff of the neck and pushing downward until the offender submitted in a belly-exposing sign of submission that says, "Okay, I get the message, I'll behave." Both dogs, having settled their differences, continued about their play as if nothing happened. Breaking down these discoveries and implementing them into my lessons with my dog-training clients made me discover exactly why my methods worked. This new discovery propelled my horse training to a whole new level; I modified my methods to suit herd or pack behavior, depending upon which animal I was working with.

I started taking in "rouge" horses, ones that were deemed vicious, dangerous, and hopeless. Once I was able to break down the cause and effect of the undesired behavior, I was able to gain the trust and respect of the horse. I discovered that there were no "bad" horses, only bad experiences that left them feeling vulnerable and scared.

A horse, by nature is a peace-loving creature that will avoid confrontation at all costs. He is also a fight or flight animal, meaning that if he's scared, he's going to run. If he can't run away from his fear, he's going to fight with all he's got. When a thousand pound animal gets his dander up, you get out of his way! Once a horse resorts to fighting, he is labeled "mean." This unfair earmark is usually a product of the very fear that he has had instilled by his handlers. In reality, these "fight" patterns are the result of insecurity caused by a misinterpretation of communication. The end result is undesirable, and often dangerous behavior that leaves both horse and owner extremely unhappy.

A perfect example of this type of training gone wrong is Slack, the horse that would make all my professional dreams come true, and become the hero in all my horse stories ever to be written. This handsome, jet-black thoroughbred was to become my Cinderella story. I met this incredible gelding while galloping a few racehorses at nearby stable on a freelance basis. I would finish up my work at my own barn, then drive the twenty minutes to gallop in order to make some extra cash.

Slack shipped in from Louisiana one day and it was rumored that he was an "un-trainable," dangerous, rouge horse with a penchant for attacking people. His reputation was that of a mean, opportunistic, beast who would attack at the slightest provocation. When I looked into the stall of the wild beast, I saw something quite different. I saw a lonely, misunderstood soul withering and dying in a solitary confinement that wasn't warranted or justified. Hidden beneath that rough layer of self-preservation was a sweet, gentle personality; I just knew it. After other riders had failed in getting him back to the track and into work again, I asked the trainer if I could give it a shot. Having nothing to lose, he agreed.

Slack became my "project" horse. People from the barn, knowing that he had a wild streak in him, would literally line up on the fence when they knew that I would be bringing the "bad boy" out for a lesson.

Slack's early lessons were spent on the ground, carefully getting to know me on common ground. It astounded people that I wasn't just throwing a saddle up on his back and climbing aboard, "showing him who was boss." Instead, it seemed as though I was simply taking him for evening strolls, going along with him during his violent temper tantrums as he flailed his front legs in the air and struck out his hooves in protesting demonstration.

I knew there was to be no rushing or pushing this horse, however. His was a temperament that would not take kindly to being pushed around. Without being told, I could see that he'd had enough of that to last a lifetime. Two deep, ugly scars on his beautiful face told me the tale of abuse and neglect that this horse had sustained, and his deep mistrust spoke volumes about the type of "training" he'd received in his past. No, this time was going to be different, vastly different. I was working on his terms now. It might take a lot longer, but I knew the rewards would far surpass any hardship on my part.

Slack's re-training came along slowly, and I was building a solid relationship with him. He even started looking for me when he heard my car pull up, or heard my voice. To everyone's amazement, he was becoming easier to handle and even followed me around like a puppy dog when I let him loose in the arena. As I had known all along in my heart, he was a marshmallow underneath that mean façade.

Finally, the time had come to put a saddle on Slack and try to get him back to the track. He eyed me warily as I buckled the cinch and led him outside to the arena, but didn't protest. Our regular crowd had gathered, with everyone taking bets as to who would win: Slack or me.

The trainer gave me a leg up and led Slack around for the first lap of the arena. Slack snorted nervously, as if he were expecting me to hurt him. My heart broke, thinking of the horrors he'd endured, and I leaned over to pat his neck reassuringly. I asked the trainer to let him go, and I steered him around the arena solo. He did fine at the walk. He was still uneasy, but he was responding to my cues and listening to my voice. I looked over at the trainer and he nodded to me and asked me to put Slack into a trot. I squeezed my legs, signaling to Slack that I wanted him to increase his pace. All of a sudden, it was as if he was released from a starting gate. He bolted and swerved violently, almost unseating me. I was able to gather up my reins and pull him to a stop where he rose to his full height on his hind legs. Once back on all fours on the ground again, he pawed the earth and snorted furiously. I patted him and talked to him until I could feel the panic leave his body. We walked around the arena one more time. He was fine. I asked for the trot again, careful to be soft and smooth with my aides. This time, he snorted, and tossed his head nervously, but remained in control.

From that first ride, Slack continued to improve. He was already broke to ride. He knew all the cues and knew what was expected of him, he was just scared that he was going to be hurt again. The horse's most vulnerable body part is his back. He can't kick, strike, or bite an enemy on his back. This is why Slack was so afraid of his rider. He didn't trust people anymore and having what he viewed as an enemy on his back terrified him. Once I'd gained his trust, first on the ground, and then on his back, everything else fell into place. He went back into training again, with me as his exercise rider.

As time wore on, I became quite attached to Slack. I'd come visit him on my days off, feed him treats, and take him for long walks. On his days off from race training, I was allowed to trade his racing saddle for an English riding saddle and hack him out in the fields. He and I both loved it. We'd wander through the fields that surrounded the farm, enjoying the freedom and companionship of one another. I would do bending and suppling exercises with him, just as I would with a horse I was training to jump. He really got into it, and I saw different muscles beginning to bulge from his athletic frame. It occurred to me that this horse would make an excellent jumper, something that I was looking for at the time, but could not afford.

I approached the trainer and asked him if I could buy Slack. With some consideration, and realizing that Slack hadn't won a single race since he'd been there, the trainer said, "Sure, you can have him for $2,500.00." With my limited funds, it may as well have been a million dollars, but he was willing to take payments on time and give me extra work to help pay for Slack. I was elated. Slack immediately came out of race training and started his new career as a jumping horse.

"You'll never get him to do it," said the trainer when he heard about my plans for Slack. "He's too rowdy and stubborn, and too old to learn another discipline." At three years of age, I didn't think Slack was too old at all. Rowdy and stubborn, maybe, but I could get him to concede; I knew I could.

I must admit, however, even I was a bit disheartened when Slack showed his intense fear of the poles we use for jumping. For reasons known only to him, he would rear up and try to bolt whenever anyone so much as moved a jumping pole. I had a feeling it had to do with his former abuse, but I'll never know for sure. In any case, there was no way to get this horse to be a jumper without getting him over his fear of the poles. I knew I had my work cut out for me, and for the first time, had the fleeting thought of finding another career for him.

It took me three months of patient consistence to get Slack to walk over a pole on the ground. It took me three more months to get him to hop over a simple cross rail, a tiny jump made with two poles placed in an X shape. Gradually, I raised the cross rail in small increments until Slack was actually jumping over it. It took me six months to get this horse to do something that most horses do in one day. I considered it a great victory.

I finished paying off Slack's purchase price and moved him to the barn where my other horses were stabled. His training was coming along nicely, and he started showing a real penchant for jumping. As the jumps got higher, he got more excited and I started to see a true athlete developing. At his first horse show, we received an eighth and fourth place finish. I was happy just to get around the course.

Everyone associated with this rouge horse knew what a huge success his training was. Each show was an improvement and we actually started becoming viable contenders. By the following season, the jumps were much higher, the competition much stiffer, and Slack started earning his own way, collecting checks virtually each time out.

Slack

Having seen what I'd done with Slack, people who had difficult horses started looking me up to work out their problems. Successfully training difficult horses nearly tripled my business. Private horse owners, who had nearly given up on their horses, brought them to me for behavior modification and were eternally grateful to me for "fixing" them. Racehorse trainers, who didn't have time for their charge's shenanigans, sent me their problem horses and spread my name all over the industry, telling their colleagues how I'd straightened out their "crazy" horse. My section of stalls was kept full, with a waiting list to get in. It was time for me to look for a bigger place and expand my business.

All my childhood experiences and sacrifices paid off when I proudly opened the Reignbow Ridge Equestrian Center. On this fifty-four acre farm, I operated a full-care boarding, training, and riding instruction facility. The farm was named after my favorite mare, Lady Reign; the Standardbred that had taken me to so many victories. By that time, she and I had been together for twenty-six years. Reignbow had been my greatest student, best teacher, and cherished friend. After her retirement from the show ring, she and I were often invited to perform riding/training demonstrations at horseshows, racetracks and other events—she's even served as mascot on behalf of our Sheriff's Department on various occasions. When I opened my own facility, I felt I had to name it after my very special friend.

Lady Reign and I at National Finals

I leased the bank-owned property that housed Reignbow Ridge for a great price. It was a run-down, over-grown piece of real estate that was up for sale, but had no real prospects of being sold. The area was being built up into residential neighborhoods, and the farm was the last rural property on the block. There was a creek and wetlands that ran smack through the middle of the property which made it illegal to develop on, and the market was soft for a run down horse farm that would take quite a bit of money and time to fix up. This was great for me, but put the bank who owned it in a precarious position because the abandoned property had been looted several times and was left wide open for such vandalism without a caretaker on the premises. I made a deal to rent and live in one of the property's two houses, fix up the stables and fencing, and operate my business out of it. They agreed to the deal, viewing it as a mutually beneficial situation.

The first order of business was to mow down the overgrown grass and weeds that had taken over the entire property. With a couple of friends' help and a few borrowed tractors, we had the place trimmed up in no time at all. Keeping it that way proved to be another matter. There was no room in my budget for a tractor, so I used a push mower to maintain the entire fifty-four acres. Sometimes it felt as if that was all I did. By the time I finished one side of the farm, the other side had to be done again. It was never-ending.

Next on the list of things to do before bringing the horses to my new place was removing the piles of garbage that had been left by the previous occupants, fix the broken fences, and clean out the stalls of the two horse barns. Again, I enlisted the help of friends and family, and within a couple of weeks, we were ready to open for business.

I literally worked from sunup to sundown every single day, seven days a week, in order to make Reignbow Ridge a success. I maintained my clientele of horses to train and picked up some boarders as well. In addition, I offered pony rides and pony parties in order to cater to the neighborhood that was growing all around me. This proved to be a great marketing tool, and brought me lots of new riding students to teach. I had never worked harder in my life.

I hired a full-time employee who helped me muck stalls and feed the horses, and I allowed a couple of the boarders to work off some of their board by assisting me with the daily chores, freeing me up to ride, teach and compete. It was a grueling schedule, and it was unbelievably difficult, but my stalls were full and I was making ends meet. I was seeing the benefits of all my hard work paying off, and I felt a sense of satisfaction and delight that I had found the courage to believe in and follow my dream. I was more determined than ever to make my dream come true.

While at Reignbow Ridge, I had two very promising jumping horses I was bringing along. My "big" horse, Reignbow Ridge's Flying Hope (Slack), and another little, yet very talented mare named Reignbow Ridge's Classy Lady. With my two self-trained horses, I was fully prepared to head down the road that would hopefully lead me to Grand Prix.

For those who aren't familiar with the lingo, Grand Prix is the pinnacle of horseshow jumping. It pits the bond of horse and rider against the course, which is made up of approximately twelve numbered jumps that are up to five-feet high and four-feet wide. The course is timed and is made up of colorful shapes and textures that are pleasing to the eye and designed to test the training and courage of both horse and rider. Add to that the ambiance and sophisticated glamour that is associated with show jumping, and you've got my dream.

One day in late summer, 1996, while competing at a weeklong horseshow, I came face to face with a horseman I had admired for years. Mark Leone, of the famed Ri-Arm Farm, was the youngest member of "Team Leone," made up of Mark and his two older brothers, Peter and Armand.

I had watched Mark on television for years, read about his victories in countless magazine articles, and had aspired to his coveted position in the horseshow world. I especially aspired to the occasions in which he was invited to represent the United States in international competition on the Untied States Equestrian Team.

Then, there he was, just a few feet away from the in-gate of my jumper class. I summoned up every once of courage I had, marched up to him and introduced myself. I told him that I was aspiring to ride Grand Prix and was looking for a coach, and would he please consider taking me on as his student? After listening to my introductory speech, asking a few questions to which he was apparently satisfied with the answers, and watching me ride Classy Lady in a qualifying class, he asked me if I would be attending the Monmouth County Horseshow in two weeks. "Yes," I said, "I'll be there." "Good," he replied. "We'll hook up there Friday afternoon to prep you for your class."

Me and Reignbow Ridge's Classy Lady (Toots)

This was it—my ticket to the big time. I had my foot in the door. One of the country's leading riders had agreed to coach me! The weekend of the Monmouth County show, I was showing my bay mare, Reignbow Ridge's Classy Lady. "Toots", as she was know around the stables, was a feisty, tiny bit of a thing with tremendous jumping ability, she also had a mind of her own and wasn't opposed to expressing herself in the show ring through bucking and other antics. As I was warming up for our pre-competition lesson with Mark, I sent a prayer Heavenward that the sassy little filly would behave herself so that we could make a good impression. Although I'm sure that God heard my prayer and sent the message to her, Toots once again proved herself to be a woman of her own mind and behaved badly, to say the least, in all three of her classes. Bucking around the course like a rodeo bronco instead of a well-trained jumper that she was supposed to be, we had rails down in every class.

I was sure that my "ticket to the big time" was going to be revoked. I felt humiliated and deflated. Of all days for her to cop an attitude! I sheepishly returned to where Mark was waiting at the rail, certain that he would admonish me for wasting his time. Instead, he told me that my mare was a real handful and liked the way I handled her, even through all the antics. We made arrangements to meet up at his farm for a lesson the following week, only I'd bring Slack the next time!

I began to trailer one or two of my horses the two and a half hours to Ri-Arm once or twice a week and take lessons from Mark. Afterwards, I would always hang out, watching other lessons, and offering to help around the barn. Soon, I was asked to exercise client-owned horses and was given impromptu lessons on them. We continued this way until March of 1998. Then, one afternoon, back at Reignbow Ridge, I received a phone call from Mark. He asked if I could meet with him and his business partner, Steve, for lunch later that week. I agreed and traveled up with Slack, planning on squeezing a lesson in while I was there.

The day of my meeting with Mark and Steve finally arrived, and we settled on a restaurant close to the barn. I still had no idea what they wanted to say to me. Nothing could have prepared me for what came next. Mark and Steve knew how hard I'd worked, keeping up my facility and driving so many hours to train. They also knew of my ambition of riding Grand Prix. They'd seen my dedication first-hand and thought I would be a great asset to their facility. Would I be interested in being bran manager of Ri-Arm Farm? Would I? Would I be interested in managing one of the East coast's most prestigious facilities? Yes! Yes, I most definitely would! I didn't even pay attention as they outlined the very generous employment package they had offered. I didn't care. All I cared about was being one very giant step closer to my dream...

* * *

The next few weeks were a blur, wrapping up things at Reignbow Ridge, arranging for my very understanding and supportive clients to be moved to other facilities, and finally moving my own things to Ri-Arm. As part of my employment package, I was permitted to keep one horse with me. I brought Slack. My other horses were boarded at a friend's farm where I would visit them on weekends. Being at Mark's facility full-time gave me even more learning opportunities and I soaked up every one of them like a sponge. He provided me with many learning experiences, giving me twice as many lessons, having me ride several different horses, and inviting me along to horseshows and other equestrian events. The job was a dream come true. Dreams are very delicate things, however, and I found out much too soon that even the best of them are not immune to disaster...

Chapter Six

Life was good. Everything was perfect. I had a great job that not only paid well, it was something I loved doing. Slack and I were really coming along, the result of all the extra lessons and training time. We were jumping bigger courses and were starting to get noticed by other competitors. In the winter shows we had competed in under Mark's tutelage, we were placing well, and more importantly, doing it consistently. I looked forward to the up and coming spring/summer show season.

I was living my little-girl dream. How lucky was I? Still, something wasn't quite right. At night when I laid in bed waiting for sleep to come, I couldn't deny this gnawing feeling that I wasn't where I was supposed to be. I remember admonishing myself, thinking, "I've got everything I've ever wanted and worked for, and still I'm not fulfilled, what's wrong with me?" I felt guilty and selfish, knowing that I had a whole lot to be thankful for. The night kept my secret and I kept pushing forward, looking for what I envisioned as success.

At Ri-Arm, I was in charge of a staff of seven girls. We all shared a very large farmhouse on the property. After work, we'd usually all chip-in for dinner or go out to eat, recounting the events of the workday. We'd also rent videos or do a little shopping at the mall. A few of the girls frequented the nightclubs in nearby New York City, and would literally "dance until dawn," arriving back at the farm just in time to exchange their dancing shoes for muck boots. I was often asked to join them, however, I'd begun to experience extreme fatigue and couldn't imagine partaking in such an outing. I no longer joined the girls for dinner, or anything else for that matter. I had all I could do to get myself showered and into bed. I was lucky if I had the energy to have dinner delivered.

I was a bit concerned at my sudden exhaustion, but figured it was the stress of moving and starting a new job. Logic threw a wrench into that theory, because even though I was still working very hard, this job did not have nearly the long hours or physical responsibilities that I had at Reignbow Ridge.

It was April of 1998, just a few weeks after experiencing the fatigue. I noticed that I was having difficulty bending down and straightening my right knee. It was proving very difficult to bandage legs and pick out hooves. Thinking I'd wrenched it or something, I rubbed it with a bracing liniment. It began to swell. I iced it and rested it as much as possible after work. It swelled bigger and got even more painful. I continued to ice it and made a mental not to have it checked out the next time I went home. Within a couple more days, I was unable to pull jeans over the swollen joint, now the size of a large grapefruit, and was in severe pain. To make matters worse, my exhaustion was overwhelming me and I started spiking high fevers. I made an appointment with my doctor. Diagnosis: Lyme disease.

I was devastated. I broke the news to Mark and Steve and told them I'd need a leave of absence in order to have my knee drained and rehabilitate it in physical therapy. The doctors said I should take at least two months off in order to give myself adequate time to recuperate and heal. Two months. It may not seem that long, but with the upcoming show season right around the corner, I needed those two months to train. Mark offered to keep Slack at Ri-Arm and keep him going for me, but I decided that the time off would probably do him some good, too. Besides, I couldn't bear being away from him for that long. I stabled Slack with my other horses, and I moved back home to my mother's for the time being, with the assurance that my job would be waiting for my return in July.

Once I'd had my knee drained and finished my two-week long treatment of antibiotic, there was nothing more to be done other than physical therapy and wait. Having been an active athlete all my life, I don't do "wait" well. With my doctor's permission, I took a temporary position as a secretary in order to help pass the time. The assignment was finished at the end of July, perfect timing for my return to Ri-Arm.

Little did I know that something, or someone much bigger than myself, had other plans in mind for me. On July 2, 1998, just a few short weeks before my planned return to Ri-Arm, I was heading home to my mother's house after visiting Slack and my other horses. I noticed some friends' cars parked in the lot of one of our hangouts. Billy's served the best Buffalo wings and ice-cold, draft birch beer soda, both favorites of mine. Since I had the car running with the air-conditioner going because both dogs were in the car waiting for me, I only stopped in for a quick visit. After sharing a couple of wings and downing a frosty mug of birch beer, I made my way back to my car and to Dewey and Brandy.

On my way out the drive, a curious thing happened. I stopped to put my seatbelt on—something I hadn't done since I was in high school in driver's education. Although very aware of the safety value of seatbelts, I had always been very claustrophobic, and could never get used to the restraint system. I never really stopped to think about how strange it was, my buckling up. I just did it and continued on my way. It is because of that one unconscious detail, which I'm thoroughly convinced, was the first evidence of one of my guardian angels at work that I'm here to tell my story. Approximately fifteen minutes later, my car was rear-ended by a tractor-trailer. In one horrible, glass shattering, metal-crushing moment; my dream, and life, as I'd known it, ceased to exist.

I still remember the impact vividly. As an incredibly loud, sickening, metal-crunching sound filled my ears and wracked my body with a painful jolt; I realized I was spinning out of control. I found myself looking at the headlights of oncoming cars, then the trails of taillights in front of me, and headlights again, until it was all a blur. I knew I was dead; I just prayed that I didn't hit another car and kill someone else. During my drive, I'd noticed that just about every car was filled with families, as was usually the case on the turnpike during a big holiday weekend. There were children in just about every car I'd seen. I thought about them and prayed. I didn't pray for myself; there wasn't time. I waited for a second impact, the one that would end my life. It never came. All the deafening noises from the crash had stopped, it was deathly quiet, and I feared the worst. My world grew hazy and I was very sleepy.

My first conscious thought was, "Where are my dogs?" I remembered feeling the vehicle spinning for what seemed like an eternity. Could Dewey and Brandy have been ejected from the car? I called to them; I got no response. I felt my heart fall through my chest. I frantically called for them again and tried to look into the back seat where they had both been. That's when I made the startling discovery that I was trapped. My seat had broken in the impact and I was in a flat, lying down position, pinned down by the driver's side door. Coming to this realization without the benefit of knowing if my dogs were still alive, caused me to panic. I started screaming for help. It seemed instantaneous that a gentleman arrived to help me. He tried to calm me down, but I was inconsolable. I vaguely remember saying over and over, "My dogs, were are my dogs? Are they dead?"

He replied by saying, "How many were there?"

"Two," I croaked between sobs, "A big, mixed-breed and a Collie."

"They're both still there," he said. "And they look to be in very good shape, just shook up." He reached his hand in the back and told me he was petting them and they were licking his hand. I thought that was very strange, as they both were very territorial about the car when I was in it. They'd never let anyone even think about putting their hand in the car before. I figured they were in shock, too, and didn't give it a passing thought until later.

"They're both sitting up looking at you; they seem more worried about you than anything. I don't even see any blood or anything. Now, you on the other hand, don't look so good. How about if you calm down so we can get you some help?" His words were music to my ears. I didn't hear anything after him telling me Dewey and Brandy were okay.

I looked up at the well-dressed man who'd come to my rescue and felt a feeling of calm envelope me. His gentle demeanor and soothing words seemed to penetrate my very soul. He took my hand and promised me everything was going to be okay. I didn't understand how he could say that, because things seemed far from okay. I knew he was trying his best to make me feel better, so I just smiled weakly in agreement. The shock was beginning to wear off and was soon replaced by excruciating pain in my head, neck, back, and my right knee; the same knee, incidentally, that had been affected by the Lyme disease. I grew tired of making conversation; all I wanted was to go to sleep.

Somewhere during that time, my rescuer pulled the door off of me, which helped to relieve some of my anxiety. (It later dawned on me that he'd had no tools, or help of any kind, something that seemed very strange and unbelievable in hindsight). He stayed with me until others had arrived, talking with me, asking me endless questions to keep me awake, and at the same time, calming me down. Another couple that had been passing by stopped to see if they could help. The woman stayed with me, holding my hand and talking to me, again, making sure I stayed awake. Her husband had called my mother, gently explaining to her that I'd been in an accident and was being taken to the hospital. He also made arrangements with her to drop my dogs off at our home, something for which I am eternally grateful.

Many police cars arrived in a flurry of blurred activity, and an ambulance arrived to take me to the hospital. I was carefully removed from the mangled remains of my vehicle. I looked for the man who'd rescued me. I wanted his name and contact information so that I could thank him later, but he was gone. The couple, which had remained, assured me that the man had given his information to the police and I could get it from the accident report. That man was never seen again, and his name never appeared on the police report. We put ads in newspapers covering the entire east coast, trying desperately to find the stranger who had come to my rescue, but no response was made. To this day, I'm convinced he was my guardian angel.

Meanwhile, everyone kept insisting that I just relax; everything was going to be okay. How could they keep saying that? I remember asking for my dogs—I needed to see them for myself. An officer picked up Brandy and brought her around for me to pet, and pointed to Dewey, who was sitting next to another officer on the shoulder of the highway. Reassured that my dogs were okay, I allowed myself to be taken into the ambulance. That's one of the last things I remember about that horrible night.

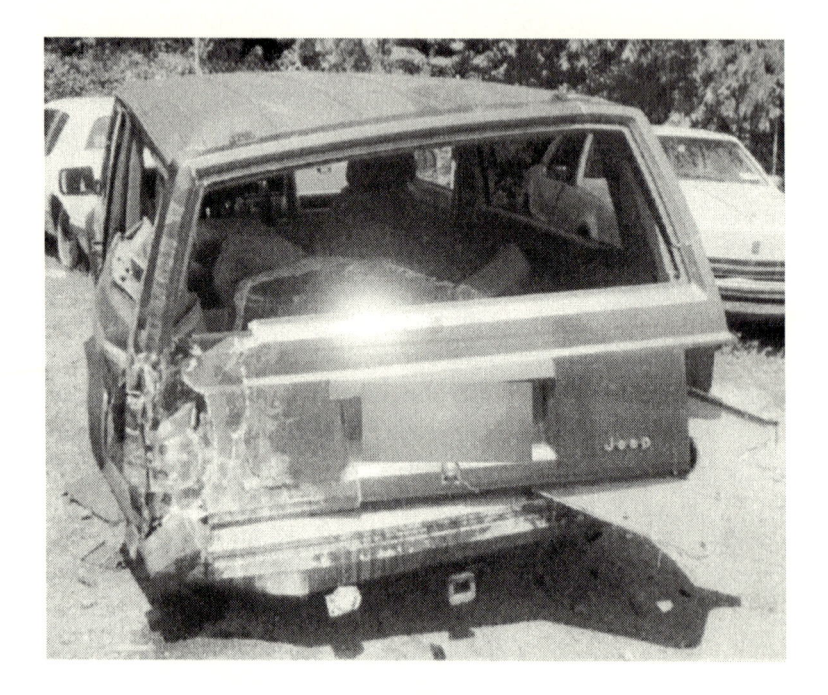

My totaled jeep

At first, it didn't seem that I was injured all that badly. As a matter of fact, I was released from the hospital the very next day. It was determined that I'd sustained knee, neck, back and head injuries in the crash. After reviewing initial X-rays, which showed minor contusions on my right knee, MRI's, which showed some disk bulges, and a CAT scan, which showed a slight bruising on my brain, it was determined that I was well enough to go home and begin rehabilitation on an outpatient basis.

I thought, "This is great, I'll be doing rehab for a few weeks, and I'll still be able to get myself together for the winter circuit in

Florida." I was really excited about getting home and back to my career. It was such a great feeling being reunited with Dewey and Brandy. They were so happy to see me, and the feeling was mutual. They had both been thoroughly examined by their veterinarian and both got clean bills of health, something that I was very thankful for. They both remained close by my side, as if being more than arms-length away would take me away from them again. I began to relax, thinking about how lucky I was and how I was going to make up for the time I was going to lose from the riding circuit. I didn't know it at the time, but my dream, and life as I'd known it, were over; shattered and mangled right there on the highway, along with a sea of broken glass and pile of twisted metal.

Shortly after I arrived home from the hospital, my progress took an unexpected and drastic turn for the worst that was far more serious than anyone could have imagined. Within a few days of my homecoming, I began to experience trouble reading and writing. Words would jump out of order and sentences didn't make sense to me. I was spelling things wrong; even my name. It was the holiday weekend, so Mom and I decided to wait until Tuesday to go back to the doctor for a recheck.

I decided to "rest" my brain, and not try to read for the rest of the weekend, and camped out in Mom's recliner in front of the television instead. As usual, Dewey and Brandy remained close by my side and I cherished the company of my canine sentinels. That Saturday afternoon, Dewey started acting very unusual, however, and was nudging me for constant attention. When I'd tired of petting him, I told him to go lay down and turned my chair around to turn my attention back on the television. Dewey not only ignored my command (he never disobeyed my commands), but he positioned himself right on top of my feet and sat down, resting his head on my lap.

I laughed at his seemingly crazy attempt at getting more attention, and was about to command him back to his place by my side when all at once, the room tilted violently and spun into a dizzying blur. I tried to cry out to my mother, who was in the kitchen, but I couldn't get my voice above a hoarse, slurring whisper.

Panicked, I tried to get up to run to her, but Dewey wouldn't let me. He jumped up onto my lap with the front half of his body and used the full brunt of his massive one hundred and twenty-pound frame to push me back into the chair. I lost track of space and time and everything became a total blur. When the room stopped spinning, and I felt my body return to normal, I became aware of Dewey's weight squashing me and his wet tongue licking my face and hands. He gently removed himself from my lap and sat staring at me, looking very worried, as was Brandy, who was lying on the other side of me. I found my voice and croaked out a cry for help, which brought my mother rushing in from the other room.

We went to the hospital, where it was determined that I'd begun having seizures. A seizure is a disturbance in the electrical activity of the brain. Most people are familiar with grand mal seizures where patients lose consciousness and their muscles twitch and jerk uncontrollably. During petite mal seizures, the type I was experiencing, the patient has a sudden loss of awareness and stares straight ahead, is unable to communicate, may blink make repetitive movements with the mouth or lips, or mumble indistinguishably.

My doctors stabilized me and referred me to the University of Pennsylvania in Philadelphia, where I was hospitalized for a week, hooked up on monitoring equipment that provided the doctors with all the data they needed to know about my head injury in order to treat it. It was determined during that time that I was also experiencing acute memory loss. I thought the year was 1996, two years earlier. I couldn't remember much about my childhood unless family and friends related specific memories to me. It was getting harder and harder to keep days in order and remember what I'd done a few days before, and there were frequent lapses in which I couldn't account for periods of time.

A deep, dark depression began to settle over me. I learned that clinical depression is often related to head injuries, as the brain's chemistry has been altered. It didn't make me feel any better to know the cause of the hopelessness. I was overwhelmed with my injuries, and my brain was contributing to feeling of loss and confusion. I felt as though I wanted to die. I was put on medication and set up with counseling for my depression, was medicated for the seizures and headaches, and was scheduled for cognitive rehabilitation to assist with my memory loss, at a facility near my home.

While I was hospitalized, my mom told my doctors about Dewey's strange behavior preceding my seizure, and though some blew it off as coincidence, others were not surprised, citing that some animals have the innate ability to discriminate the change in brain chemistry that occurs during certain neurological events, such as seizures. I thought back to the day that I'd saved Dewey from being put to sleep and it dawned on me that he'd just returned the favor.

Back home, things got harder and harder. I was always angry it seemed, something that was not in my nature. I was angry at the world. It seemed like the simplest tasks were demanding and it didn't seem to be getting any better. I had trouble speaking. I was always slurring my words, mixing them up, and finding the right word for the right application proved to be impossible. I would make cognitive mistakes like putting the milk in the cupboard, confusing products (i.e., I once mistakenly used air freshener instead of hair spray because the cans felt the same in my hand), and once even left the oven on with cookies baking inside. They were smoking and about to catch fire when my mom discovered them and came to my rescue. I'd completely forgotten that I'd been baking and went off to do something else. I felt stupid and helpless.

In the weeks that followed, my neck and back injuries that had started healing normally began to get really painful and I experienced numbness and tingling in all of my extremities. By the end of the year, I had significant loss of feeling from the chest down. The doctors couldn't explain why this was happening, and I started a barrage of intensive testing that would drag out over the next two and a half years.

They couldn't tell me what was wrong, but they kept telling me that my broken body just wasn't healing. For some reason, I just got worse. It was theorized that a virus, perhaps somehow related to the Lyme disease, had set into the injured joints and was taking advantage of my weakened state, but that was never proven. Nothing was being explained. I was getting sicker and sicker and they couldn't do anything about it. The pain was indescribable and was literally driving me crazy. I was on a variety of medications for pain, none of which really worked. I was drowsy and dopey all the time from the pain meds, so they gave me other pills to wake me up, and still others to maintain my brain chemistry.

I lost my driver's license due to my medical condition, and wouldn't be able to apply for it again until my seizures were under control. Not that I could drive anyway, because I would get lost trying to figure out where I was going and how to get there. I was still having seizures on a regular basis as the doctors tried to find the right combination of drugs to control them. I also developed an intense reaction at my loss of control during my seizures. A paralyzing fear of being attacked in my prone condition kept me from going anywhere, or being anywhere alone. I became a virtual recluse, a prisoner to my disabilities.

I was struggling in cognitive therapy, trying to relearn how to memorize by using my other senses, and to speak, read and write properly and effectively. It was grueling and frustrating work. I knew I was fighting against time, as they told me that whatever memory I was going to get back, I'd have to have retrieved within the first year. Anything past that would remain lost forever. The fear of losing even more of myself pushed me through the frustration and I worked as hard as I could.

While I could fight to regain my speech and memory, there was nothing I, or anyone else could do about my pain. I was losing my mobility. My legs were weakening to the point of collapse and even the shortest of distances exhausted me. I started walking with a cane, and leaned on furniture and walls to get around the house. Eventually, I found myself in need of a wheelchair for outings and some chores around the house. *I'm going to get better*, I told myself. *Better than I was before. The doctors didn't know what they were talking about. I'm strong. I'm determined. I'm an athlete. I can overcome this . . . can't I?*

Chapter Seven

I was in denial. In the months that followed, realization set in and it was apparent to me that things were never going to be the same again. How could this be? I'd worked so hard, only to have everything taken away from me just as it seemed it was well within my reach. Going from an active athlete to someone who needed assistance with the most mundane things was too much for me to handle. My world became one of fear and uncertainty.

I had always classified myself as a rider. Period. I put all I had into training, riding and competing. I ate, slept and breathed riding. I was a good rider, yes, but without that, who was I? I didn't know and that scared me. Not to mention, the never-ending, hideous pain that wracked my broken body twenty-four hours a day, seven days a week. There was no getting away from it; even through the haze of the multitude of painkillers I was given, the pain nagged at me and slowly drove me insane.

Another thing I lost following the accident was my boyfriend of a year and a half. A handful of good "friends" weren't far behind; all of them saying that it was, "Just too hard to see her like that." It wasn't that easy seeing myself "like that," either! It's true what they say about finding out who your true friends are. My best friend from the time we were little girls, Eileen, was the only one who remained by my bedside, wheelchair side, and finally by Dewey's side, to offer her unending love and support. We remain the very best of friends to this day.

The following are a few poems that were written shortly after my accident (I actually tape recorded them until I was able to write adequately again). It was during the time that I was still struggling with reading and writing, trying so desperately to hold onto everything that I had left, (including the boyfriend):

High Stakes
©1999 by Kimberly Carnevale

*Sitting close together,
yet still a world apart.
His stoic silence deafening;
broken only by my heart.*

*He says that he still wants me,
yet he pushes me away.
Casual indifference
keeps his love at bay.*

*He lets me cry alone—
never tries to understand;
all I need is a warm embrace
at the least, a gentle hand.*

*Sometimes I feel it's wrong to touch him—
like I've crossed some blood-drawn line.
I feel starved for his affection—he refuses to accept mine.*

*His words, they often wound me—
deep into my core;
yet the desire to reclaim our love
keeps me coming back for more.*

*He's keeping so much from me,
something deep inside.
If he really loves me;
why the need to hide?*

*At one time he proposed to marry me,
then like his love, he took it away.
I gave it some time
to let him make up his mind,
but this game's getting too hard to play.*

The stakes are high, I stand to lose it all—
it's a game I can't afford to lose.
It's now or never—cards down or forever—
I'm forcing him to choose . . .

Shortly after showing him this poem, my boyfriend confessed that he was holding back from me and broke up with me, explaining that I was just going through too much and he couldn't handle it all.

It began to occur to me at this time that I would never find love again. Trapped in a body that refused to heal, I remember sobbing to my mother one lonely night, "What man is ever going to want me like this?" I don't remember her answer; just her loving arms and compassionate understanding that have always been there without fail throughout my ordeal.

My writing, which had always offered me solace, was difficult and frustrating at best. Letters jumped and twisted in indistinguishable fashion in my injured brain. Try as I might, I simply could not read, or write. This was a devastating last blow. The deep, dark depression that had settled over me took complete and total control over my afflicted state of mind, and I lost my will to live. So deep was my depression, that I refused to take the help that was being offered to me by doctors and therapists. Instead, I wallowed for nearly a year in self-pity and anger. I just couldn't seem to find the strength or determination needed to pull myself out of that deep, dark, pit of despair. One dark day in July of 1999, just a few days after the anniversary of my accident, in a dissident fit of hopelessness and physical and mental agony, I swallowed a large mixture of my painkillers. I wasn't thinking at the time that I wanted to kill myself, just that I needed that maddening pain to go away. I needed just a little while of being free of pain to recoup recharge. I just couldn't take it anymore.

The next poems are ones that were written (actually voice recorded), just before the overdose, when I was grasping at anything that might make the pain go away; even if just for a little while. My cry for help is heard loud and clear in them:

Life Song
©1999 by Kimberly Carnevale
All rights reserved

> *What happened to my big, white horse*
> *racing the wind to carry me away?*
> *Why can't my mind remember*
> *the tools I used only yesterday?*
>
> *So many dreams*
> *faded away so fast;*
> *so many dreams*
> *locked away so deep in my past.*
>
> *The door I closed shut*
> *just a short time ago*
> *is begging to be opened-*
> *I'll find the real me there, I know!*
>
> *Nightmares scared me*
> *from what I thought was reality;*
> *now I envision my future*
> *the way I want it to be.*

*No more living
for someone else's dreams-
I've finally discovered
what freedom really means.*

*Once I though
I was just a big mistake-
but now I truly realize
exactly what's at stake.*

*A soul is given
only one precious chance-
one heart to beat, one dream to live,
one very special song to dance . . .*

Whose Eyes Are Crying My Tears Tonight?
©1999 by Kimberly Carnevale
All Rights Reserved

Whose eyes are crying my tears tonight?
I swore I'd never give up,
but now I'm losing this fight.
Stilled words and emotions of a broken heart,
shards of a life left torn apart—
tell me, whose eyes are crying my tears tonight?

These feelings are tearing me up inside,
I can't express them, but I can no longer hide
the bitter pain locked away so very tight;
oh, tell me, whose eyes are crying my tears tonight?

My past is clouded in a deep, dark haze;
faded memories of brighter days.
The future holds such uncertainty—
why can't I remember who I used to be?

Fighting the pain won't make it go away,
it's starting to take over, more every day.
I'm riding a wave of mixed up emotions
that go higher than the sky and deeper than the oceans . . .

Someone from Above must have had another plan,
the easy road forsaken, down the troubled one I ran.
But somewhere down that road, I lost my strength to fight—
let the Heavens rain down on me and cry my tears tonight.

These feelings, they scare me—no one understands...
I can't control them any longer, I'm no longer in command.
I want this nightmare to be over, want to dream a dream tonight—
troubled heart, so afraid, whose gonna cry your tears tonight?

I don't understand these feelings inside,
where do they come from, why won't they die?
I want to come in from the storm and return to the light—
I want to cry my own tears tonight...

Hold On . . .
©1999 by Kimberly Carnevale
All Rights Reserved

>Won't someone please help me?
>I'm losing what I fought
>so hard to hold onto.
>
>Opposing forces getting stronger,
>I can't hear my heartbeat any longer—
>won't somebody please help me?
>
>I remember times,
>not so long ago
>I was on my way to better things.
>Fate stepped in to lend a hand,
>I'm no longer in command—
>someone please help me, I'm falling.
>
>I struggle to fight the daily fight.
>I can no longer see the light,
>pain has taken over.

My dreams, they drift away on silent breezes,
which linger for a moment to offer
some glimmer of hope,
only to be pulled cruelly out of reach once more.

I refuse to settle, it's just not in me.
I have to save me . . .

The pain I bear is unending,
sometimes even maddening.
But I know in my heart, I know in my soul
I will get through this and reach my goal.

Hold on, spirit, hold on heart! Hold onto your dreams—just hold on . . .

I had wanted to go someplace where the pain couldn't touch me—at least for a little while. Where I went was to a place that had a great, white light. Bathed in this incredible, soothing light, I knew I'd found the peace I was so desperately searching for. I also knew I couldn't stay. I saw the paramedics working on my body, pleading with me to respond, but didn't want to go back. The pain was gone—I wanted it to stay gone. Something told me that I couldn't stay, though. I woke up two days later in the Cardiac Intensive Care Unit with wires sticking out all over and a tube down my throat. It didn't even occur to me to mind. That was when it hit me that I must be really sick.

The nurse that was assigned to me ran and got the doctor. As they removed the tube from my throat, I vaguely remember him telling me that I was one very lucky young woman. I didn't feel so lucky at the time. He told me that they really had to fight to keep me alive. I remember wanting to tell him that they shouldn't have done me any favors. He said that the average patient in that particular unit was sixty-years old and the average length of stay was two days. I was thirty—years old and my stay on that unit lasted a week.

I was so angry. I was so angry that they had the nerve to rob me of my peacefulness. I dared them to make me better. I didn't make it easy; I didn't want to get better. I realized then that I really did want to die. I was angry with them for saving me. I was angry with them for subjecting me to the horrible pain again. I was angry at everything.

They finally allowed my family to come in. One look at my Mom's face and all my anger melted away in feelings of guilt, remorse, and an overwhelming sense of failure. A parent should never have to go through what my poor mother did. I was so wrapped up in my own pain that I couldn't see the pain of others around me.

I remember a story that I have to chuckle at in retrospect. My best friend, Eileen, relates this story, as I really have no clear recollection of it. Anyway, she came to see me during those first days, and taking in all the machines, wires, and other gadgets I was attached to, she was at a loss for words. Finally, she came up with, "Just remember that God never gives us more that what we can handle." She said I never skipped a beat before I choked out, "Well then I'm really impressed with who He thinks I am!" My attitude was sour—plain and simple. Look where it got me. It was somewhere during that time that I remembered my time in the white light and realized my recovery was up to me and only me. The doctors, nurses, and other medical staff were there to show me the tools to use, but it was ultimately up to me to implement them.

I emerged from the hospital three weeks later with a renewed sense of incredible faith, spirit, courage, and determination. I was going to put everything I had into my physical and cognitive rehabilitation and stop fighting the ones that were trying to help me. What else could I do? Trying to cop out didn't work. There was no place to go but up. It didn't get much lower than this. I had truly hit my rock bottom. Now I was making a commitment to life instead of death. I was going to reach out for every ounce of strength that was being offered to me by friends, family, and loved ones. I was going to use my newfound faith to push me through the pain and I was going to succeed in this, the biggest fight of my life.

Fortunately for me, I didn't have to embark on that journey alone. My dog Dewey was the key that set me free from my disabilities and together, he and I set out on a most-amazing journey...

My four-footed angel, Dewey

Chapter Eight

From the onset of my seizures, Dewey reacted to them *before* they started by sitting on my feet. He is one of the rare, talented individuals who can alert to impending seizure activity. Scientists recognize this behavior, yet are still baffled at how they are able to do it.

It wasn't long before I noticed a difference in myself when I realized Dewey was there for me. I wasn't as scared anymore. Dewey didn't "flip out" when I had my events like people are prone to do. His quiet, loving demeanor kept me calm and his stimulating licking of my hands and face helped to bring me out of the event. And because of his massive size (120lbs), I felt very safe and secure with him by my side. Afterwards, he'd lay down on my bed with me until I'd slept off the exhaustive effects of the passing seizure.

Not only did I feel safe because of his massive size, but also I was able to utilize it to assist me when I was still in my wheelchair, and eventually, with the implementation of a special harness, lean on him while I was "learning" how to walk again. He shouldered a lot of my weight when my pain was too much for me to bear, and gave me incentive to keep trying. Around the house, Dewey was a Godsend. I got stronger, mentally and physically with his help. I felt as though I had an ally against my disabilities. It somehow made it easier to manage.

One day, I was watching a television program and it showcased a young woman who had epilepsy and utilized the assistance of a seizure-alert dog. Her dog was able to detect her oncoming seizures by sitting on her feet, or whining at her. I excitedly called my Mom into the room. She and I stared at the screen in amazement. That dog on television was doing exactly what Dewey did prior to my own events! I learned that seizure-alert dogs, also referred to as service, or assistance dogs, were considered medically necessary, and were permitted by law in all places that the general public was allowed to go. They are covered under the Americans with Disabilities Act (ADA), a federal law that protects the rights of persons with disabilities. An idea came to me and I was very excited. I was going to find out about having Dewey trained as a service dog.

I took Dewey to a service dog-training center to have his skills evaluated by professionals with the hope that by having him certified as a service dog, I would regain much of the freedom I'd lost. It was determined that he was, in fact, alerting to seizure activity. However, the cost of training Dewey professionally was very steep and well out of our financial limitations. At first, I went home and started to fall back into my self-defeatist attitude. I was angry that my freedom was being pulled out from under me again. I felt the grips of depression trying to wind its icy grip around me again.

Just when I was about at my wit's end, I heard a voice from deep within. Another idea jumped into my head and I decided to take on Dewey's training myself. I was confident that I could utilize my animal behavior skills to train Dewey to help me full-time. I found a service dog training center in the mid-west that allowed me to train Dewey to do specific tasks that assisted me with my disabilities, videotape his progress, and mail the tapes to them for approval.

On January 6, 2000, Dewey received his service dog certification (*note: service dogs are not required to be certified, it is handler's choice*). We'd done it—together. The dog I'd saved came full circle to save me right back! The journey that we had yet to share together was nothing less than a miracle . . .

Throughout my recovery, Dewey remained faithfully by my side. He accompanied me to all my doctors, including specialists in New York City and Philadelphia, always providing assistance and reassurance. During particularly painful procedures, he would sit by my side and offer me comfort. Holding onto him and looking into his sympathetic, brown eyes helped me take the focus away from my pain.

When we weren't visiting doctors, Dewey accompanied me to hockey games, restaurants, movies and shopping excursions. He was always the perfect date! His selfless assistance gave me a whole new outlook on life, and motivated me to pull myself out of the grips of depression and seek the help that was being offered. Getting past the hurdle of depression was the biggest step I would ever take in my recovery. Keeping me out of that depression was a job that Dewey performed flawlessly.

This is a poem I wrote about Dewey:
©2001 by Kimberly Carnevale
All rights reserved

> *I thought I was saving him,*
> *in what seems so long ago.*
> *Yet he'd be the one to rescue me,*
> *little did I know.*
>
> *This "mutt," he stole my heart,*
> *left there all alone.*
> *For eighteen months, he knew no love-*
> *chained to the porch that was his home.*
>
> *I gave him love and shelter.*
> *Fixed his wounds and kept him fed.*
> *Gave him toys and Milk Bones®,*
> *a family and a bed.*
>
> *He fit right into my lifestyle,*
> *went to work with me each day.*
> *Filled my life with fun-filled memories-*
> *ones I cherish most today.*
>
> *The crash changed who I am today,*
> *I'm not the same old "me."*
> *Chained to my own aggressor,*
> *this time it was the mutt who set me free.*

*Dewey waltzed right through my fears
and put his needs aside
to fill my world with light again
and fill my heart with pride.*

*This once-abandoned pup
is now my closest friend.
He escorts me through the game of life
and shows me there's no end.*

*No end of life, of victory;
just a shadow of a doubt-
took me beyond the darkness of despair
to the land I'd heard about.*

*This four-footed angel was sent onto me,
of that, I'm almost sure.
He opened my eyes to the beauty inside-
little things I'd never noticed before.*

*Four-foot devotion was sent onto me,
to strengthen and raise my soul.
He helped my body start healing,
my heart to start feeling
and made my spirit whole.*

*Each day when I reflect
on who I was back then,
I see the master plan unravel
to bring me my closest friend.*

*A friend on which to lean on,
who'll never turn his back on me;
a friend who showed up just in time
to set my spirit free . . . .*

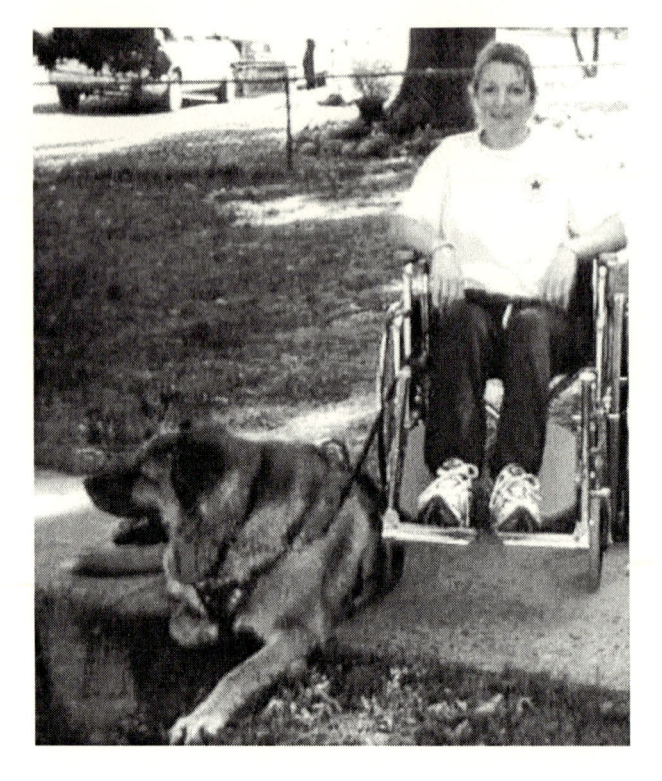

I love you, Dewey!

Another thing that was keeping me out of the pit of depression was my newfound faith. Although I've always been a member of a church, I've never considered myself to be a really religious person, more of a spiritual one. Following the overdose, I learned that keeping my spirit alive and well nourished was a key factor in maintaining my physical well being. That newfound piece of information was instrumental in my focus and recovery. I began to see what I had, instead of what I'd lost, or didn't have. Whenever I started to complain about something, I thought about other people who had it much worse than I did. When the pain got really bad, I would turn to Dewey, and allow him to soothe me and take my mind off myself for a while. During those times, I would pray to God and ask him for the strength to overcome my challenges. In return, I would thank Him for all the gifts in my life. I knew I'd experienced a revelation of some sort, but was so affected by it, that I didn't know how to express it.

There was nowhere to go but up. I'd almost killed myself, it doesn't get much worse than that. From that point on, whenever I felt as though I couldn't carry on, I would just think of that horrible, dark place where I'd come from and I'd dig in and force my mind to run in a different direction with a determination that I didn't think humanly possible. What else could I do? My options were limited: live or die. I'd already chosen to live. With that choice I'd made a promise, one that I didn't take lightly.

I saw things with so much clarity. The little things that tended to upset and bother me in the past didn't matter anymore, and the things that did (family, friends, and spirituality), I grabbed onto with a whole heart and committed every nuance to memory, locked away forever to cherish. Birds sang so much sweeter, and flowers smelled more fragrant. The sun shone brighter, both in the sky and in my heart. I'd found inner peace.

I experienced a sense of control over my situation. When things got real bad, I would pray. The time that I spent in prayer quieted my fears and capped my emotions, allowing me to deal with issues with a clear state of mind. I found that if I used the same tunnel-vision mental focus that I'd used as an athlete, it could get me through just about anything. Dewey provided any fortitude that was needed after that. Things were definitely looking up. I was ready to meet this new life head-on, rising up to whatever challenges that it presented, knowing that with God's and my dog's help, that anything was possible.

Dewey, proudly sporting his new backpack with his hard-earned certification card attached, accompanied me wherever I went. I marveled in my newfound freedom. I wasn't afraid to go places alone. I wasn't afraid because I knew that as long as Dewey was by my side, I was never alone.

I thought my troubles were over. Little did I know, they were just beginning. While I'd already overcome tremendous obstacles on this rough road I was traveling, I was about to learn that there were several more bumps waiting for me just around the bend.

Chapter Nine

Shortly after I began taking Dewey into public places, I was confronted by access denial. Employees and storeowners would refuse to allow me to enter their establishments with Dewey. At first, I was embarrassed. I was still getting used to being seen in public with this new body of mine that didn't quite work properly. I wasn't comfortable in my own skin; I guess you could say. Red faced, I'd stammer that my dog was an assistance dog and I'd fumble to relate the ADA, list all of my disabilities and how Dewey helped me. After several minutes of harassment and degradation, I was usually "allowed" in and would sheepishly continue on my way.

For the most part, my disabilities are invisible. This has been a major cause for access denial; I don't "look" disabled, therefore, it is wrongly assumed I do not need a service dog. You can't see my brain injury, arthritis, cognitive problems or seizure disorder; but just because they aren't visible does not mean they do not exist. There are times I can walk pretty well; other times, I limp or am in a wheelchair due to arthritis and Fibromyalgia (a chronic, widespread muscle and soft tissue disorder). I have worked very hard getting my speech back to an acceptable level, but I still have problems with word finding and recall; and often stutter or slur. My brain gets overwhelmed very easily now, causing debilitating panic and intense emotional overload. My arms and hands often go numb and have a tendency to weaken, causing me to drop things frequently. All of these conditions are in some way met by and alleviated with the assistance of my service dog.

As time wore on, and I became more adept at handling confrontation, the embarrassment turned to anger. Anger that I couldn't express, because in doing so, I'd be making matters worse for the next service dog team that followed me. One particular pain-filled evening, I entered a store hoping to pick up a couple of sale items and get right out. I was in so much spinal pain I could hardly walk or breathe and I was leaning on Dewey heavily for mobility assistance. It was then I experienced the access denial that topped all access denials.

It literally took me all morning to get to the shopping center in order to stock up on some necessities. I gave a sigh of relief when I saw the store employee at the second set of doors, thinking he was going to hold them open for me, as it was blatantly obvious that I was struggling and in a lot of pain. Instead of the greeting I'd expected, he delivered a rant of foul-mouthed obscenities, the gist of which I was able to discern (leaving out the profanity), that I had to be out of my mind to bring that huge dog into a store. I stared at him, stunned for a moment, with tears that threatened to fall. Then, from somewhere deep inside, anger unlike any I'd ever experienced before bubbled up and spilled out in a self-defensive declaration. I straightened my shoulders with a painful wince and looked him right in the eye. Willing my injured brain and slurred speech to cooperate I stated, "Look! I am a person with disabilities and this is my service dog. In accordance of state, local, and federal law, this dog is considered medically necessary and it is my civil right to be accompanied by him in all places where the general public is allowed. You have violated my civil rights by denying me access, not to mention offending me with your foul-mouthed insults. I am in a considerable amount of pain right now and I don't have the time or energy to deal with your insults or your close-minded attitude. I noticed a police car in the lot outside. If you are so sure that I'm crazy, and that I can't bring my dog in this establishment, why don't you go and get one of the officers to come inside and settle this? I'll be shopping, page me if the police need me. Oh, and by the way, before you jump all over someone just because they're different, you might want to take a minute to examine the faults within yourself that makes you so insolent." I got a loud ovation and a couple of "you go girl's!", from the crowd that had gathered, held my chin up, and continued shopping with Dewey by my side.

On the way out of the store, the guard came over to me and apologized. Apparently, one of the other employees who'd heard about service dog law had filled him in on his illegal behavior and told him he could be in a lot of trouble. I was still stung by what he'd said, but I accepted his apology and left. I got out to my car and cried. A lot. I cried because I hated being talked to like that. I hated that I wasn't able to instill in that young man's mind just how much it took for me to even get to the door he attempted to slam in my face. I cried because I couldn't think of anything better to do about it.

Late that night, I was awoken by an idea. It suddenly occurred to me that there was one common denominator in all access denials: lack of education. Armed with an arsenal of researched information and my usual determination, I vowed to make something good come out of my accident.

I was going to go back to all the places that had denied me access and teach them about the Americans with Disabilities Act and other laws that protected the rights of persons who utilize service dogs. I was going to let people know how instrumental Dewey was in my recovery and share with them the wonderful gifts service dogs bestow upon their disabled partners. I was going to help end access denial, one door at a time. I was facing a daunting task, yet I knew now that I could do anything with my service dog by my side.

My accident changed not only what I did; it changed who I was to become. I lost a cherished dream, but Dewey gave me the courage to pursue a new one. In March of 2001, the headlines of our local paper read, "Dog saves his rescuer in turn. Woman crusades for the acceptance of service animals with a program called, Canine and Abled™. Local and tri-state television stations did feature stories about us and I was invited to speak about the program on a television talk show. My phone rang off the hook after that. Schools wanted me to speak to their students, boy/girl scout troops booked programs, civic and service organizations wanted to hear all about what I was doing for disability rights. My prayer had been answered and I had a new dream. Dewey and I were going to make good come out of a shattered dream; we were going to make a difference because together, we were Canine and Abled™!

Dewey helped support me when I was rehabilitating my weakened legs

Chapter Ten

My vision for my program was one of local, basic, service dog education. If I could hold open just one door for one other service dog team through my teaching, then I would have done my job. So focused was I on the educational aspect of the program, that I left out the details of my story and how Dewey and I became partnered to begin with. Then one day, I was contacted by a pastor of a local church who'd read about Dewey and me in one of the newspapers that had covered our entire story. This is what he wanted me to speak about. He said it would be good to include some service dog law, but what he was primarily interested in having his parishioners hear about was our inspirational story.

Inspirational? I never thought about our story that way before that. He told me that by maintaining my faith and overcoming my challenges I was an inspiration to others, and it would make my audience feel more hopeful about the trials in their own lives if I shared with them the intimacies of my recovery. I still wasn't entirely convinced, because I couldn't see myself as being an inspiration to anyone. I was an ordinary person put in extraordinary circumstances. I did what I needed to do to survive.

It actually put more pressure on me, trying to come up with something that would move my audience, not just educate them. Service dog law was factual. It was well researched, and I had it down pat. Presenting an inspirational speech was going to call on emotions and memories that I wasn't certain I was ready to revisit, much less share with a room full of strangers. However, I was eager to promote my program anyway I could and I went along with it, rewrote my note cards, and with Dewey steadfast by my side, delivered my first "inspirational" speech.

Standing on that podium, looking out over the expectant faces waiting for me to give them something that I wasn't convinced that I could, I went cold. I was back to being the second-grader, who when called upon in class to recite an oral report, got tongue-tied and stammered unintelligibly throughout the entire thing. I looked down at Dewey, lying obediently by my feet where I had commanded him to a few minutes before. What was I doing there? I was so unprepared. What was I going to say? I really didn't know, but I wanted it to at least be intelligent. Dewey looked up at me and I leaned over to scratch his head. I'd always felt as though I could do anything with him by my side. I faintly heard my introduction over the wild beating of my heart and focused my gaze Heavenward, sending a prayer to help me get through.

My introduction ended and I heard myself saying, "Hello. My name is Kimberly Carnevale and this is my service dog, Dewey. Prior to becoming disabled I was a professional athlete vying for a spot on the United States Equestrian Team. Prior to becoming my service dog, Dewey was a stray dog with lots of love to give, but no one to give it to. We both came together to "heel" our wounds and together have embarked on a most-remarkable journey. I'd like to share our story with you today." And so it began. The rest of the speech remains a total blur. I only know that during that hour, I was able to include service dog education in my speech and made my audience laugh, cry, and most importantly; think. Think about what was important in their life, and plant the seed of hope, instilling the belief that they already possessed the ingredients to make that hope grow.

During the applause and standing ovation that followed, I realized that once again, my prayers had been answered. I prayed for the words, and they were provided. I wasn't speaking; I was being spoken through. I felt rejuvenated and overjoyed. The ovation that I received that first night was better than any I'd received at any horse show. I realized afterward that it was better because I was in it for other reasons than my own. I'd helped others find hope, and in helping others, I was given a precious gift in return. I looked Heavenward again to give thanks. This time, I thanked

God for giving me a new direction and a new dream. I thanked Him for allowing me to turn my tragedy to triumph.

After receiving such positive feedback following my first inspirational presentation, I realized that I was in a unique position to do even more than I'd originally thought. I set out on a mission to instill the hope and courage in others without them having to go through the tremendous pain and loss that I had undergone. If I could do that, if I could help others find the tools to overcome their own challenges, it would take out some of the tragedy of my accident. If I could reach even more people, and maybe prevent someone from going over the point of no return, then it takes the senselessness out of my accident. I could live with that.

Human beings need to figure things out. We all want to know why things do what they do. We need to know why things happen when and how they do. It was no different for me in the days, weeks, months, and even years following my accident. I wanted, actually, it was more like, I needed to know why. Why did my dream of riding on the Team get pulled out from under me just as it was about to take wing? Why did I have to go through so much after losing what I thought of as "everything"? I know I've found my answer in sharing my story with others. By accepting what we are given, then giving of ourselves to others, we are rewarded far beyond our expectations. I often think back to the nights at Ri-Arm when I wondered what was missing from my life. I know I've found it now, and I know that I'm exactly where I'm supposed to be. This program fulfills me in ways that I never dreamed existed.

Chapter Eleven

At the age of eight, Dewey was beginning to show signs that it was time for him to retire. He would often lie down if we were waiting in a line, he took longer to rise, and one day I noticed a slight wobble in his hips. A trip to the vet confirmed my fears—Dewey was developing arthritis. I made the heart-breaking decision to retire him by the end of 2001.

I began to prepare Dewey for his retirement by letting my family members "spoil" him in ways that were never permitted before. He was allowed to take long walks with the neighbor's children, go fishing with my friends, go for car rides with my brother, and other activities that didn't involve me. In the meantime, I was busy looking for a protégé to take over. It wasn't easy! After a six-month long search, I found Dawson; or rather, he found me . . .

My first Collie, Brandy, who'd since passed away from old age, had been the deciding factor to determine that there would be no other breed choice for my next service dog. I'd been conducting an intensive nation-wide search and had reviewed the aptitude of approximately a hundred and sixty dogs before a local Collie breeder who'd know about my search contacted me bubbling with excitement. "I've got the perfect dog for you!" she gushed. "He's in Pennsylvania, only four and a half hours from here. He was bred by one of the nation's top Collie breeders to be a show dog, and showed tremendous promise, only his bite didn't line up perfectly. His breeder is heartbroken, as he bred the dog for himself. He wanted to find him a home, but is very attached to him and won't let him go to just anyone. Dawson is sweet, loving and extremely intelligent. Kim, this is your dog, I know it!"

I tried to absorb all that the breeder had said, thinking to myself that this didn't sound like "my dog" at all. I had been looking for a female, one to two-years old, and preferably sable in color. At seven months old, the only requirement Dawson met was his color. Still, something nagged at me and I was persuaded to go meet him and test him in person.

There was a number of aptitude "tests" that I put the dogs I was interviewing through. These tests gauged a wide range of behavioral and intellectual attributes of the dog, and gave me a pretty good idea of how well she, or in this case, he, would take to training, distractions and the million other stressors that are all part of a service dog's life.

Prior to visiting Tartanside Collies, I spoke with John Buddie, Dawson's breeder, over the telephone. We spoke at length about the pup's personality and attributes and by the time we finished, I was very much looking forward to meeting the little Collie dynamo. John told me he would be away at a dog show the day I was to come visit, however, his business partner, David Supplee, had agreed to show me around. When I went to the kennels to meet Dawson, I was given the grand tour of the facilities. I met his grandparents and his father (Tartanside Select), his mother, (Tartanside Foolproof), was away with John at a dog show. Then David brought out Dawson. I felt my heart jump. "Stop it!" I warned myself. "Don't fall for a pretty face, this dog is going to be your lifeline. He may look good, but does he have what it takes?" I had a duffel bag with me, stuffed with lots of things that looked scary, made noises, and other implements designed for aptitude testing. I had intended on doing ten different tests. I did three, including a retrieval test, which Dawson excelled at, and told David that the puppy would be going home with me.

Any doubts I had about his immaturity, gender and aptitude quickly blew away on the quintessential whirlwind that is Dawson. His zest for life and sheer delight in learning new skills was entirely contagious and the insecurities of starting a new partnership blew away with my misgivings.

Dawson took to his training like a champ. He worked side-by-side with Dewey for several months, learning new skills and developing self-confidence and finally moved into the position of my full-time service dog. He has already been awarded several certificates and awards from various organizations, honoring his service to mankind, and he continues to earn my respect in his outright mastery of his job.

His repertory quickly grew, as his great intelligence begs for constant challenges. Dawson's humor and great love for life has not dimmed with his growing maturity. It is a cherished trait that I try to nurture and take great delight in; it has been a lifeline because it's what keeps me from falling into the dark, evil grip of depression that is always waiting for complacency and the opportunity to take hold of me. Dawson is a bright light of hope shining into my soul, shattering the threat of darkness, and lifting me up to give me the ability to follow a new dream.

Canine and Abled's Dawson

Chapter Twelve

Service dog education is key to preventing access denials and other rude behavior. This chapter covers basic service dog education and gives answers to some of the most frequently asked questions that I get about my service dogs. I truly hope that by providing such needed education, it will help hold open a door or two for other service dog teams.

Dawson and I during a Canine and Abled™ presentation

Service Dogs 101

The federal civil rights law, the Americans with Disabilities Act (ADA, Title III, 28 code of Federal Regulation, section 36.104), defines a service dog as any animal that is individually trained to help a person with a disability. (*Note: the disability might not be visible*).

Service dogs (sometimes referred to as assistance dogs) help their partners in many ways. Seeing-eye dogs and hearing dogs are the most widely recognized assistance dogs, but there are dogs that benefit a wide range of persons with disabilities associated with many diagnoses, including, but not limited to:

- Arthritis
- Spinal cord injury
- Head trauma
- Multiple sclerosis
- Seizure disorders
- Muscular dystrophy
- Recovery from trauma or depression
- Anxiety
- Neuroses

Many patients reported some or all of the following health benefits after being partnered with a service dog:

- Lowered blood pressure
- Moderation of stress
- Decreased serum cholesterol
- Mitigation of the effects of loneliness
- Psychological well being
- Increased self-esteem

In my own case, I've:

- Been able to stop taking all anti-depressants and anti-anxiety drugs

- Had an increased sense of well-being and burst of renewed self-confidence
- Been able to set new goals for myself, knowing that with God's and my dog's help anything is possible!

Tasks Accomplished By Service Dogs

Service dogs are trained to reliably accomplish many tasks associated with many disabilities. Most people know that seeing-eye dogs guide the blind, but not many are aware that there are service dogs that alert to impending seizure activity, lowered blood sugar, heart attack, and even environmental allergens.

Psychiatric patients have reported a decrease of problematic symptoms after being partnered with a service dog. Other dogs are trained to help with daily living such as helping put clothes in and take them out of a washer and dryer, turning lights on and off, opening and closing doors, retrieving dropped items, assisting with dressing and undressing, and other everyday tasks that would prove to be impossible without this very important assistance.

Dawson assists me in different ways than Dewey did. Since I haven't had a seizure since I've had him, we don't know if he will alert, however, during "make believe" training sessions, he's been taught to stay with me and remain by my side in the event that I am unconscious or in an altered state. He also alerts me if I've left the oven or stove on, the water running (something I do all the time), or candles burning unattended. When I'm in increased pain, he retrieves things for me, opens doors, and brings me objects from all over the house, including a cold drink from the fridge, or the telephone in case of an emergency.

Due to my brain injury, I have frequent panic attacks, and during these episodes, Dawson is taught to automatically climb into my lap and give me a "Collie hug." His nearness is comforting and if I pull him to my chest and close my eyes, I can put my breathing in time to his and ease my attack.

Dawson looking over his awards during a presentation

What Breeds Are Used For Service Work?

Service dogs may be of any size, breed or mix of breeds. Males and females are both used in service work. Breed and gender are not as important as the personality and adaptation of an individual dog. Some dogs are better at some things than others. Not all dogs are good retrievers, just as not all will be able to alert to impending physical changes of their handler. It takes a special individual with the right temperament and disposition to be able to reliably perform tasks in situations that most dogs find intimidating and stressful.

Many dogs are rescued and retrained in order to assist persons with disabilities. Others are bred for certain desired qualities. Still others, like Dawson, start out in one career, and find that their talents lie elsewhere.

The time it takes to train a service dog depends on the individual. Training continues throughout the dog's career so it is never really "over." Service dogs are constantly taught new things and practice old tasks daily in order to keep them fresh and interested. I teach Dawson many new tasks because his intelligence begs for stimulation. Learning new things is a lot of fun for him, and me too!

You Can't Bring That Dog In Here, Can You?!

Because service dogs are specially trained and considered medically necessary, they are allowed to go where most dogs are not. They are permitted in stores, restaurants, and all other public places where the general public is allowed. Even when an establishment has a "no pets allowed" sign, they must permit access because service dogs are not pets, they are specially trained animals that perform specific tasks for their partners. Service dogs are also permitted on buses, trains, airplanes and all other modes of public transportation.

There is a federal law called the Americans with Disabilities Act that protects the rights of persons with disabilities who rely upon the assistance of service animals. Under this law, it is illegal for a person to be denied access, be turned down for an apartment with a "no pets" policy, or otherwise discriminated against due to his/her disabilities.

The Americans with Disabilities Act

The Americans with Disabilities Act (ADA), is a federal law that prohibits discrimination on the basis of disability in employment, state and local government services, public accommodations, commercial facilities, transportation, and telecommunications. Violation of this law is considered a felony and is punishable by stiff fines and criminal prosecution, including jail time.

Federal (ADA Title III, Section 28 CFR 36.302), and state laws protect the rights of individuals with disabilities to be accompanied by their trained service animals in buses, taxis, trains, restaurants, doctors' offices, stores, parks, housing, and all other public places.

Under the ADA, businesses that serve the public are prohibited from discriminating against individuals with disabilities. The ADA defines a service animal as ANY guide dog, or other animal individually trained to provide assistance to an individual with a disability. The ADA prohibits discrimination on the basis of disability. Violation of the ADA is considered a felony and is punishable by stiff fines and criminal prosecution, including jail time.

What Would You Do?

Suppose for a moment you are a storeowner with a "no pets" policy. A person just entered your facility accompanied by a service dog. Now what do you do? What would your employees do?

What about this one...

What questions may a proprietor or employee *legally* ask a person with disabilities that is accompanied by a service dog if they are not sure that the animal is, in fact, a service dog?

Okay, one more...

One of your employees (let's call him John), notices a person entering the establishment with a dog. Thinking that he is acting in the best interest of his employer, John confronts the person and makes them leave, even though the person claims to have a disability that is mitigated by their dog. The person with a disability files a claim with the United States Department of Justice...

What do you think the consequences of John's actions will be? Will he do jail time or have to pay a fine? Would you, being the owner of the establishment, be penalized for John's lack of understanding of disability rights?

If it appears the animal is trained and is paying attention to the individual with them, then making a challenge and confrontation is not in the best interest of the business. Making a false charge against someone with a disability accompanied by an assistance animal is defamatory and an act of discrimination.

Most state laws covering the use of service animals involve criminal prosecution. Penalties can carry over to the owner of the establishment for failure to ensure his/her employees are versed in disability law. Individuals are becoming savvy to their rights granted by state and federal laws and they are learning how to enforce them. Business owners' ignorance of disability rights does not constitute denial of those rights. It is strictly the owner's responsibility to learn the laws and prevent their employees from raising barriers to equal access.

Business Rights and Responsibilities

When a service dog team enters an establishment, the proprietor or employee may ask the following questions if they are unsure the team is a service dog team:

- ➢ Are you disabled?
- ➢ Is that a service dog?

These are the only questions that can be asked. Requiring "proof" of disability or proof of certification or licensing of the service dog is illegal. Asking what disabilities a person has is defamatory and illegal. Some people may not feel comfortable sharing their disabilities and it is their right to retain privacy in such matters. Remember, not all disabilities are visible.

Other Laws That Pertain to Disabilities

Federal laws which protect individuals with disabilities include the ADA, the Fair Housing Amendments Act of 1988: Sect. 504 of the Rehabilitation Act (1973), the Air Carrier Access Act (1996/90) and other regulations. These laws protect the rights of a disabled person to use a service animal in apartment buildings, on airplanes and all other public places that don't normally allow pets.

How do I recognize a service dog?

Generally speaking, a service dog usually wears a cape, backpack, harness or other accessory identifying him/her as a service dog.

There is no law, however, that requires this so this is only a rule of thumb.

Unfortunately, there are some people who think it's "cool" to be able to take their pet dog with them into public places, so they unlawfully pass their pet off as a service animal. This is not only illegal; it is downright dangerous. Pet dogs are not conditioned to handle the things a service dog has been carefully trained to, such as shopping carts, elevated noise levels, lights, children, and other unexpected stressors. Dogs who are overwhelmed by such things can act out with aggression or fear.

People who think it is "cute" to bring their pet dog in public and lie about it being a service dog put the entire service dog community in jeopardy of access denial because their misbehaved dogs give real service dogs a bad reputation. Please, on behalf of all service dog teams, do NOT pass off a pet dog as a service animal!

A Day In The Life Of Denial (Access denial, that is) . . .

Imagine for a moment that you are disabled and rely upon a service dog. You are looking forward to getting out of the house for a while to take advantage of a great sale you'd read about in the weekend circular. You get up, get into the shower while your dog lies patiently alongside the tub in case you drop something or help is needed. You get dressed with the assistance of your canine friend, humming to yourself with the anticipation of shopping for yourself. You've been planning for this all weekend, because nothing is done on the spur of the moment anymore, you have to wait until your body is going to cooperate with you and "save up" the energy needed to go out.

You amble out to the car (with the assistance of your dog), and embark on what you hope will be a productive shopping excursion. With your dog lying quietly in the back seat, you drive the few blocks to the shopping center; cringing and gasping at every single bump and crack in the road that sends excruciating bolts of pain through your body. You fight back the tears, concentrating instead on the joy of shopping for yourself.

You and your well-trained service dog, who himself (or herself) has been down a long road to EARN the title of service dog, is dressed in a walking harness and/or backpack with large, highly visible patches that distinguishes him/her as an assistance animal. You approach the door that literally took you all morning to get to, expecting to be greeted politely by the employee standing next to it. Instead of the greeting you expected, he/she delivers the statement, "Hey, you can't bring that dog in here!" You are frustrated at the rude, degrading tone, however, you calmly explain the state and federal laws that protect the rights of service dog teams. You even produce an educational brochure for the employee's review, but this is futile, as this person has already deemed you unwelcome.

You choke back your anger and frustration and insist on speaking with the manger, who is just as uncooperative as the employee. Determined to exercise your civil rights, you refuse to leave. The police are called and a scene is created, with people viewing YOU as the perpetrator of some gross misdemeanor.

To your relief, the officer explains the situation to the store management and you are now "allowed" to enter the store, but it is quickly apparent that security has been heightened all around you. You become acutely aware of the employees following you and watching your every move. You are sent sidelong, disdainful glares as you go from section to section throughout the store.

The trip you had looked forward to, and fought so hard for, isn't nearly the uplifting experience you had hoped for. Exhausted by all the stress and feeling uncomfortable from the added security which makes you feel as though you've done something wrong, you return back home, and back to the prison of your disabilities with one more shred of dignity stripped away.

Think this couldn't happen? Sadly, this story is based on actual events. Even sadder is that it isn't a localized occurrence; this happens to many service dog teams every single day, in every part of the country.

And Now, A Word From The U.S. Department Of Justice:

The Civil Rights Division of the U.S. Department of Justice and the National Association of Attorneys General has formed a Disability Rights Task Force to promote and protect the rights of individuals with disabilities.

"We have found that many businesses across the country have prohibited individuals with disabilities who use service animals from entering their premises, in many instances because of ignorance or confusion about the animal's appropriate use. Deval L. Patrick (Assistant Attorney Civil Rights Division, U.S. Department of Justice), and Scott Harshbarger (Attorney General State of Massachusetts; President, National Association of Attorneys General).

The Disability Rights Task Force helps to promote and protect the rights of individuals with disabilities.

Commonly Asked Questions About Service Animals In Places Of Business
(As outlined by the Disability Rights Task Force)

"What are the laws that apply to my business?"

Under the Americans with Disabilities Act (ADA), privately owned businesses that serve the public, such as restaurants, hotels, retail stores, taxicabs, theaters, concert halls, and sports facilities, are prohibited from discriminating against individuals with disabilities. The ADA requires these businesses to allow people with disabilities to bring their service animals onto business premises in whatever areas customers are generally allowed.

"What must I do when an individual with a service animal comes to my business?"

The service animal must be permitted to accompany the individual with a disability to all areas of the facility where customers are normally allowed to go. An individual with a service animal may not be segregated from other customers.

"I have always had a clearly posted "no pets" policy at my establishment. Do I still have to allow service animals in?"
Yes. A service animal is not a pet. The ADA requires you to modify your "no pets" policy to allow the use of a service animal by a person with a disability. This does not mean you must abandon your "no pets" policy altogether, but simply that you must make an exception to your general rule for service animals.

"My county health department has told me that only a Seeing Eye or guide dog has to be admitted. If I follow those regulations, am I violating the ADA?"
Yes, if you refuse to admit any other type of service animal on the basis of local health department regulations or other state or local laws. The ADA provides greater protection for individuals with disabilities and so it takes priority over the local or state laws or regulations.

"Can I charge a maintenance or cleaning fee for customers who bring service animals into my business?"
No. Neither a deposit nor a surcharge may be imposed on an individual with a disability as a condition to allowing a service animal to accompany the individual with a disability, even if deposits are routinely required for pets.

"Am I responsible for the animal while the person with a disability is in my business?"
No. The care and supervision of a service animal is solely the responsibility of his or her owner. You are not required to provide care or food or a special location for the animal.

* If you have further questions about service animals or other requirements of the ADA, call the U.S. Department of Justice: 800-514-0301 (voice) or 800-514-0383 (TDD).
Commonly Asked Questions compliments of the U.S. Department of Justice.

ADA Violations And Penalties

The following are just two examples of companies in violation of the ADA and the penalties that were imposed upon them. Stiff punishments are being handed down to offenders of the Americans with Disabilities Act. Not all proprietors are aware of their responsibilities to their disabled customers. Unfortunately they are paying a high price for their unfamiliarity with disability rights.

Department of Justice vs. Arizona Shuttle Service

In a complaint filed by an Arizona woman, dated March 26, 1997, the Department of Justice took action against the Arizona Shuttle Service for refusal to offer reasonable accommodations for a person with disabilities who was partnered with a service dog. The company's policy stated that only seeing-eye dogs were permitted.

In a settlement agreement, the Department of Justice ordered that within 45 days, the company was required to post a written revised policy statement declaring that all service animals, not limited to seeing-eye dogs, are welcome on company buses, cars, in terminals and offices, and any other place where the general public is allowed.

The company was also ordered to implement (at its own expense), an employee training procedure to ensure all people with disabilities, including those with service animals, would be treated in a non-discriminatory manor and are afforded the same services and courtesy as that of any other customer.

It was further ordered that Arizona Shuttle Service pay $10,000.00 damages to the woman who filed the complaint, and $5,000.00 to the United States for civil costs. In addition, the company was ordered to pay all attorney and legal fees. Those fees were separate and apart from the damages they were required to pay.

Department of Justice vs. Budget Rentals

In a complaint filed October 7, 1992 against Budget Rentals, it was claimed that three blind shuttle passengers were told their seeing-eye dogs must be crated in order to transport.

In a settlement agreement, the Department of Justice ordered a nation-wide implementation of employee training procedures. These procedures included, but were not limited to: the company, nor its employees may require proof of certification or licensing of any service animal. They may not require any service animal to be separated from its handler at any time.

It was further ordered that Budget pay each of the complaint-ants $6,000.00 in damages. In addition, records dating back four years were being carefully reviewed and it was decided that any complaint-ant within the time indicated would be rewarded no less than $5,000.00 each. The United States is entitled to seek civil penalties and their appropriate relief.

Service Dog Etiquette

A person with disabilities who uses a service dog becomes a high-profile person, not usually by choice. However, in order to help gain acceptance, and in an attempt to maintain a low-profile, he or she has made sure that their dog has met the training criteria necessary to become a safe, non-disruptive, service animal and they adhere to stringent grooming practices to ensure cleanliness. In return, service dog handlers appreciate the general public showing respect for them, as well. The following are a few etiquette tips that apply when meeting up with anyone with a service dog.

- Never call to, make noises or reach out to a service dog. This distracts the dog, whose job it is to be a medical assistance device. Without knowing it, you could be putting the handler in danger.
- Do not feed, or attempt to feed a service dog. These dogs are given carefully measured, balanced meals that help to meet their nutritional demands at specific times during the day to ensure peak performance. In addition, hand feeding a dog leads to begging, which is a major offense in service work.

- Please do not point at or whisper things about a service dog team. Not only is this rude, it is embarrassing, both to the handler and yourself.
- Please ask before petting a service dog; and don't be upset or angry if the answer is "no." Service dogs perform a very important role to their handlers, and they need to pay close attention at all times.
- Don't exclude someone with a disability from activities, even physical ones. Ask them if they'd like to join you and find out how you can accommodate their challenges. (There are often times when I am unable to participate in physical activities, such as softball or running, but I sometimes will allow Dawson to join in my friends' games; watching him having fun is fun for me!)
- Unless specifically asked, do not try to assist a person with a service dog. Assistance is the dog's job. It's much easier on a person's pride to ask their dog to do something for them; even if it may take longer to get the task done.
- Try not to get frustrated at the amount of time it may take for a person with disabilities to accomplish a task. Having a disability means that it may take longer to do some things, for example, paying for something in a checkout line. Having an assistance dog makes most everything possible, yet a person with disabilities may require extra time. Take a deep breath and please be patient.
- Not all handlers want to share the origin or details of their disabilities. Respect their right to privacy. If they do share, don't tell them you're sorry. They don't feel sorry for themselves and they don't expect you to either. People with disabilities can lead full, happy lives.
- Teach young children about service dogs and the etiquette that is appropriate when approaching a service dog team.
- Treat service dogs and their handlers the way you would like to be treated, you can never go wrong by doing that!

Chapter Thirteen

In searching for acceptance for service dog teams everywhere, I have learned many valuable lessons. I have learned that reaching for a dream is not only about obtaining a goal; but enjoying the entire journey. While I am curious to see where this dream will lead me, I am thoroughly enjoying each aspect of its growing splendor. I love learning about the business end of my program and pushing myself to be a better speaker and communicator. I love working with my dogs, always learning and trying to teach Dawson new and innovative things that will move my audiences. I love learning website design and graphic arts, both used in producing my handout and marketing materials. I love coming up with new ideas that will propel Canine and Abled™ to even further heights. Mostly, I love and am deeply grateful for this second chance at life that I've been given.

My dogs have made many things possible, things that only a short time ago would have been impossible. Yet mine is only one story in many that will never be told. There are many service dog handlers that face the same degradation, rude behavior, and uneducated insults that I have; only they won't, or cannot speak out for themselves. This is why this book and service dog education is so important! I implore of you to pass on what you have learned in this book to children, teachers, business owners in your neighborhood, and others who will benefit in this very important information, knowing that in doing so, you may be holding open a door for a service dog team, or making life easier for a person with disabilities.

At the time of this writing, the year is 2004, nearly six years after that fateful day in July that ended my career. Not too long after the conversation that I had with my mother about finding a man to love me; I met, fell in love with, and decided to spend the rest of my life with someone who accepted me as I was, supported me in my dreams, and believed in my abilities. In early spring of 2001, I discovered I was pregnant. We were so excited! This was something that I was told would be impossible after my accident. While the thought of carrying another life inside of my broken body scared me, I couldn't wait for my baby to be born. I knew that God had graced me once again, with a gift much better than I could have imagined. My pregnancy was high-risk, but went extremely well. So well, in fact, that I regained all the feeling in my arms and legs, and for the first time since the accident, was able to walk unassisted. My doctors are still baffled by my "instant" recovery, for they were looking at only accident-causing repercussions. However, since many other symptoms have surfaced, they believe that the trauma of the accident unleashed a dormant condition and have further speculated that the hormonal changes of pregnancy put a previously hidden autoimmune disease into remission.

On November 9, 2002, I gave birth to a beautiful baby daughter we named Sarah. Unfortunately, her father and I were no longer together. He lost the battle with his own disease of alcoholism and slipped back into the world of addition without so much as good-bye. The breakup was devastating to me, as it occurred when I was about four months pregnant, but I continued to hold onto my faith that one day, when the time was right, I would eventually find someone who would be willing to share my life, no matter what. I put that thought in the back of my mind, because at that time, my only concern was raising my daughter.

I face many challenges being a single, disabled, parent. But the challenges only serve to make me stronger, and I know I'll be a better mother because of those challenges. I constantly remind myself to keep positive in the face of hardship and hold steadfast to my faith, knowing that I will be rewarded for my ability to stay the course and remain in truth. It's not easy. But as I've said before and I'll say again, nothing worth having is ever easy.

Fortunately, I have the unending assistance of my family and friends, for without which I would be completely lost. Right after Sarah was born, I took up country line dancing, something that I had always wanted to learn. The low-impact, fun, exercise actually strengthened my muscles and helps keep me mobile and limber. Learning the new steps pushes me cognitively, as well. What is most important about my dancing, though, is that I've met several great, new friends that I cherish and who help to keep me going; even when I don't feel like I can. They have lifted me up, pushed me to my limits, and supported me in good times and bad. My brother, Sarah's beloved "Uncle Ricky", has been instrumental in allowing me to continue my dancing by babysitting on "boot scootin'" nights; something for which I am eternally grateful!

Me, My brother, Rick and Sarah

My daughter is an absolute joy and is a constant reminder of my commitment to stay the course of positive thinking and maintaining my faith through the storms that life casts upon me. I love looking at life through her eyes and I am very excited by what I see. Her zest and curiosity of the simple things in life is refreshing.

Sarah has a great love of animals, and they seem to take to her equally as well. It is glaringly apparent that she shares her mother's gift for communicating with them, even at this very tender age. She rides without fear on the front of my saddle, always trying to steal the reins out of my hands to steer by herself!

Dewey is relishing his retirement, taking well to life as a couch potato. He takes time out of his "busy" schedule for special appearances and presentations. He and I still take time for "just us," and he and Dawson share a special relationship as well. They both love and are very protective of Sarah, who is now a year and a half old, and she adores them as well!

At the time of this writing, I remain able to walk unassisted, though I still have lots of pain from arthritis. It's a different kind of pain than what I'd experienced before, though. While this pain is constant as well, it is tolerable and responds to over-the-counter medication. Since my accident, my immune system is considerably weaker and I am prone to bronchitis, pneumonia, and viruses that hit me often and very hard. I've also been diagnosed with Fibromyalgia, a muscle disorder that causes significant pain/stiffness, Grave's Disease, a fairly common thyroid disorder, and Lichen Sclerosis, a rare skin disorder that some think may have links to Lyme disease. As was speculated during my pregnancy, it appears that there is some sort of autoimmune disease that is lurking about, causing many of these symptoms; including the former paralysis. I am currently undergoing more testing to try to find out what that may be, as it appears that whatever remission I was enjoying is ending and I'm slowly developing the same symptoms that crippled me a few years ago. I remain positive, try to exercise regularly, and am fighting with everything I have against this unseen foe.

I am able to ride my horse for pleasure, always careful not to overdo it. I always have to be careful lifting things and carrying objects, as my neck and back will never be as strong as it once was. Getting the proper amount of rest and nutrition is key in keeping my injuries at bay. I live each day with this in mind, thankful for each day that I'm able to walk and hold my daughter in my arms.

In addition to Canine and Abled™ engagements, I am currently working on another book, the first in a series of children's books designed to teach younger readers about the wonderful benefits service dogs provide for persons with disabilities. The series goes on to point out that though we may look, talk, or seem different on the outside; we all remain pretty much the same on the inside.

I look back on how this whole thing started and thank God for the gifts He has bestowed upon me; in particular, two four-footed gifts named Dewey and Dawson.

Me, Dewey and Dawson in woods

Chapter Fourteen

Starting over... How do you begin? Good question. I asked myself that very question millions of times throughout my recovery. The answer? One day at a time. If I couldn't handle a whole day, I'd break it up into seconds, minutes, then hours until I had a handle on the overwhelming process of putting my shattered life back together.

It was never easy, it still isn't. Nothing worth having ever is. From my years of intense training, both physically and mentally, I learned to put aside negative thinking and bring positive self-talk to the forefront of my vocabulary. I often fall back on my athlete mentality, pushing myself through the pain and frustration knowing that "the gold" lies just beyond... only now, instead of pushing for a medal, I'm pushing for my life; a new life. One I hadn't chosen, but have no choice but to live out. What else could I do? Lie down and wait to die? Been there, done that it isn't at all what it's cracked up to be.

Misery is a choice. Think about it. Dwelling on things that you have absolutely no control over and playing all the "if only's" and "what if's" only serve to prolong misery and self-destruction. Believe me, I know! I played every single scenario of my fateful night on that highway over and over in my head until I sank to a level of depression that I simply wanted to die.

Can you beat that? I wanted to die. I wanted to give back the tremendous gift God had given me just because things didn't go the way I had intended them to what a spoiled brat I'd become! One day, I woke up to the realization that I had so many wonderful gifts and I took the time to examine what I DID have, instead of dwelling on what I'd lost. I asked God for His forgiveness and to please let me know how I could serve Him while starting over...

One evening, I went to a shopping center and was involved in an access denial that left me in tears. The security guard had literally cursed me out and berated me in front of the entire store. I was mortified, but I held my head up high and stood up for my civil rights and myself. With my chin up, Dewey by my side, and pride firmly in place, I finished up my shopping and left the store.

I got out to my car and cried—a lot. I cried because I hated being talked to like that I cried because that man could never know what it took for me to get to that door. I cried because I wanted to fix it, but I didn't know how. Somewhere in the middle of the night, I was awoken with a start. I saw a vision and knew my prayer had been answered.

I saw Dewey and this program as a vehicle to help end access difficulties. I saw myself speaking about service dogs and disability rights. I saw myself visiting the wards that I had been hospitalized in; lending hope and support to patients, who like me, had given up on life. In short, I saw Canine and Abled™.

That was quite a while ago, and since then, I have frequent talks with God. I ask Him what He wants from me, not the other way around. I've found that by using the gifts that He has given me to help others benefits me in ways that I could never before have imagined! I am at peace now. Oh, I still have lots of pain, frustration, and feelings of helplessness every now and then; after all, I am human. Those are the times that I thank God the most. I thank Him for all the gifts in my life and for the realization that nothing is forever and good times with family and friends should be cherished and savored. I thank Him for the constant reminder that life isn't always what we want it to be, and in those times, it is most important to rely on our faith to get us through. Throughout this journey, I've learned that blessings come to us when we least expect them; challenges come just when we think we can't take anymore, and miracles happen when we have faith in everything we do.

My dogs have been my saving grace. They have the ability to get me out of bed on the days that I just feel like giving up and giving into the pain. They get me laughing, just when I feel like I'll never smile again. They are a gift I cherish and thank God for everyday.

I used to dream of being up on the podium, accepting my gold medal while the National Anthem played in honor of my victory. The podium I see today is draped with a white and blue Canine and Abled™ banner. Instead of a gold medal, I'm presented with the ability to instill hope and inspiration in others, and my new anthem? *"I **will** survive!"*

Chapter Fifteen

Don't ever give up!
Life's lessons learned the hard way . . .

Canine and Abled™ Presentation

From the time I was a little girl, I'd set out to be the rider I'd always dreamed of. I knew I'd be on the Olympic Team one day. I'd worked hard, trained hard, and was completely dedicated to becoming the rider of my little-girl dreams. It was all within my reach . . . so close I could feel it.

But that dream wasn't meant to be. Something, or someone bigger than myself had other plans in mind for me. The day of my accident not only changed what I did; it changed who I am. I've said from the very beginning of my ordeal that there had to be a reason for my accident. It was that belief that got me through the pain, the tears, and the frustration of learning a new way of life; a life that I hadn't chosen for myself but had no choice but to live out. I gained comfort in my faith and felt that I would be made aware of the reason behind my abrupt detour from my dream when the time was right.

It took nearly three years of searching for the reason behind my tragedy, and I believe I've found it in Canine and Abled™. I'd set out to end access difficulties, yet through this program I've been able to touch many souls with my story. It has been an incredible journey, one that is still unfolding-one I've been blessed to share with two very special friends named Dewey and Dawson.

It's true that I've been faced with many challenges since my accident. Challenges I didn't think I'd be able to overcome, challenges that still plague me to this day. But I've learned something very important, something that I feel the need to share with others:

You can *never* give up, no matter what life throws your way. Even when the dream you hold closest to your heart is shattered, you need to find a reason to hang on. Throughout my ordeal, it has become glaringly apparent to me that while I may not have control over what happens to me, I do have the ultimate control of what I do about it. This is what makes me a stronger person. I've also discovered that life has its challenges that are designed to test us. Have you ever noticed that just when you think you can't take anymore, something else happens to you? Instead of taking the low road and thinking negatively during these trying times, we must find that one little part of us that simply won't give up and keep trying. It is when we pass that hurdle that we discover a new part of ourselves; a stronger one. If you ask any bodybuilder what rep builds the most muscle and tone, they'll tell you it's the last one that you push through that makes you stronger.

We can't expect to grow without challenges. Life is not designed that way. I like to think of life like a video game. I picture myself as the brave, little character running around, frantically trying to avoid the pitfalls of one screen in order to get to the next level. But even after enduring falling rocks and seemingly insurmountable hurdles, my character is given another chance; another chance to live and reach the next level. By giving in to our problems instead of facing them head on, we don't ever give ourselves the opportunity to grow—to get to the next level. It is hardship and pain that pushes us there. Think about it . . . if there were no hardship, (i.e., falling rocks, hurdles), the video game would hold little interest in playing. Life's the same way. Hardships come and go; it's up to us what we choose to do about them . . . let us beat us down or use them to make us stronger . . . I choose to be strong!

Sometimes we can't see our dreams when we are so deep in despair. It is in these times that we need to repeat over and over what we want to envision, even if we can't quite see it yet. "Fake it till ya make it!" is a common mantra many athletes use to describe their "never-give-up" tunnel vision that propels them to greater glory. Even if you don't believe that the something you are working towards is going to happen, you need to repeat it to yourself with conviction over and over again that it will; especially in the times when you least believe it. You can't reach for the stars if you're only aiming for the rooftops! Often we need to adjust our focus because we have so much trouble holding on. We need a reason to keep going . . . my reasons were Dewey, Dawson, and this program I now hold so close to my heart. This is something that I could never before have imagined myself doing; now I can't imagine doing anything else. My dogs and I are trudging down a long road in search of acceptance and understanding for service dog teams everywhere. Separately, we all had other lives, ones that were filled with hardship and uncertainty. But together, we are making a difference, because together we are Canine and Abled™!

Together, we are Canine and ABLED!

Thank you . . .

In an attempt at opening doors for service dog teams, I have traveled a road that has been graciously paved by fortitude that came in the form of cards, prayers, and awards from my audiences. The gifts that have been bestowed upon me mean so very much; in difficult times they have served as balm for my wounded spirit. The awards and words of encouragement mean more to me than any trophy or ribbon I ever won on the equestrian circuit because they tell me that I've made a difference in others' lives.

There are children who have told me that they will never give up on their dreams and adults that have told me I have inspired them . . . They always thank me profusely . . . to these people, I say "Thank you". Telling my story has been an important step in my own recovery. Hopefully I've imparted a bit of understanding along the way.

If by sharing the priceless lessons I've learned throughout my ordeal opens doors for service dog teams, helps someone find the strength to get through their own tragedy, or gives someone the courage to make their dream come true; then my accident becomes a blessing. The senselessness of it all diminishes with my ability to instill hope; this is a gift that I can give to many. If something I've said helps another human being in any way, then I receive a special gift, too. So to Canine and Abled™ audiences everywhere, Thank *you* for letting me share."

In Closing . . .

I'm often asked what my service dog does for me. My answer? He gives me freedom-freedom to go where I want, to do what I want, when I want to do it. It is a gift he gives freely, it is a gift he gives gladly, and it is a gift I cherish and thank God for everyday.

When confronted with access denial and other rude behavior, I wish I could instill the offender's mind the tremendous loss I've suffered, the long, arduous months of painful physical therapy, and the fear that I'd never be "normal" again.

me speaking at Petapalooza

I think back to the question, "What does your dog do for you?" I look down at this noble creature by my side and I say, "My service dog has restored my freedom, my self-confidence, and my ability to become a contributing member of my community. It is because of him that I was ABLE to start this program. It is because of him that I'll be ABLE to make a difference. It is because of my service dog that I'm ABLE to take the "Dis" out of disabled!"

E-mail us: Canineandabled@aol.com
WE'RE ON THE WEB!
www.canineandabled.com